UtP 10/02

Happy Father's Day
Love done June 15/03

D1118647

WHEN THE *wild* COMES *leaping* UP

Personal Encounters with Nature

EDITED BY *David Suzuki*

David Suzuki Foundation

GREYSTONE BOOKS
Douglas & McIntyre Publishing Group
Vancouver / Toronto / New York

Collection and introduction copyright © 2002 by David Suzuki
Essays copyright by the authors

02 03 04 05 06   5 4 3 2 1

All rights reserved. No part of this book may be reproduced, stored in a retrieval system, or transmitted, in any form or by any means, without the prior written permission of the publisher or, in the case of photocopying or other reprographic copying, a licence from CANCOPY (Canadian Copyright Licensing Agency), Toronto, Ontario.

Greystone Books
A division of Douglas & McIntyre Ltd.
2323 Quebec Street, Suite 201
Vancouver, British Columbia V5T 4S7
www.greystonebooks.com

David Suzuki Foundation
2211 West 4th Avenue, Suite 219
Vancouver, British Columbia V6K 4S2

NATIONAL LIBRARY OF CANADA CATALOGUING IN PUBLICATION DATA

Main entry under title:

When the wild comes leaping up

Copublished by: David Suzuki Foundation
ISBN 1-55054-964-2

1. Nature—Literary collections. I. Suzuki, David, 1936– II. David Suzuki Foundation.
PN6071.N3W43 2002   810.8'036   C2002-910862-4

Library of Congress Cataloguing information is available.

Editing by Nancy Flight
Jacket and text design by Val Speidel
Jacket photograph by Corbis/Magma
Printed and bound in Canada by Friesens
Distributed in the U.S. by Publishers Group West

The title of this book is taken from an essay entitled "Home" by Beth Powning.

Greystone Books is committed to reducing the consumption of old-growth forests in the books it publishes. This book is one step toward that goal. It is printed on acid-free paper that is 100% ancient-forest-free, and it has been processed chlorine free.

The publisher gratefully acknowledges the assistance of the Canada Council and of the British Columbia Ministry of Tourism, Small Business and Culture. The publisher also acknowledges the financial support of the Government of Canada through the Book Publishing Industry Development Program (BPIDP) for its publishing activities.

Contents

Introduction

HARVARD ECOLOGIST EDWARD O. WILSON coined the word *bio-philia* to describe our "need to affiliate with other species," a need he believes is encoded in our genetic makeup. As one example of bio-philia, he cites the fact that every year more people in North America visit zoos than attend all professional sports events. Biophilia can also be seen in an infant's instant fascination with a flower, spider, seed, or butterfly (often accompanied by a desire to stuff the object into her mouth). Yet a child of six or seven who encounters a beetle, slug, or nettle is likely to respond with fear, revulsion, disgust—biophilia transformed into biophobia.

Throughout history, every society has known that we are deeply embedded in and dependent on nature. People have understood that everything is connected to everything else and that therefore every action or inaction has consequences. Many of our songs, prayers, and rituals affirm that embeddedness and dependence and offer a commit-ment to act properly to preserve nature's abundance and generosity.

In the past century, humanity has undergone a stunning shift in the way we live that has profoundly altered our relationship with the natural world. At the turn of the twentieth century, most people on Earth lived in rural villages. We were an agrarian species. In a mere one hundred years, cities have exploded in number and size, and we have been transformed into a species of big-city dwellers. In such a human-created environment, we are surrounded primarily by other people, selected domesticated plants and animals, and a few pests that refuse to yield to our all-out war against them. A city is radically diminished in biodiversity.

I have been asked in all seriousness, "Who needs nature?" As we have shifted our domiciles to large cities and come to live with a vast array of technological wonders, it's not surprising that we would begin to regard the natural world as a frill, something removed from us to enjoy on a hike or camping trip. I discovered the consequences of this attitude a few years ago when I was host of a children's television series called *The Nature Connection*. We took two ten-year-old children, a boy and a girl, from upper-middle-class Toronto homes to a farm north of the city and for two days filmed them playing with the animals, milking cows, gathering chicken eggs, feeding the pigs, and riding horses. On the third day, we took the children to a slaughterhouse, where the boy burst into tears when he learned for the first time that hot dogs and hamburgers are the muscles of animals.

We have become further disconnected from nature by the constant recession of wilderness as our cities expand into farmland, forests, and wetlands. Highways and roads serving our love of the car crisscross the countryside and reduce the number of places that remain wild. As well, our knowledge of the world comes primarily from the electronic media, which replace the illusion of connectedness with fragments of information devoid of context or history that indicates how it all hangs together. The immense advances of science and technology reinforce the sense that our enormous intelligence and technological dexterity enable us to escape the boundaries of nature and manage our own destiny.

As we enter the twenty-first century, beset by tremendous disparities of wealth both within and between nations, terror and violence, and a single global notion of economics and progress, the natural world is disappearing at a frightening rate. I have attended a number of international meetings on biodiversity where scientists documented a terrifying rate of extinction and loss of habitat around the world, thereby upsetting the ecological diversity and balance that have enabled life to be so resilient for millions of years. But in our infatuation with our technological and economic "progress," we seem blinded to the implications.

There are those who argue for the protection of wilderness primarily because it may contain medicines, new foods, resources, and so on. Some say it is simply a matter of setting proper economic values for parts of nature—that is, getting the pricing right. But I believe in the end that preservation of the wild is not about accommodating economics but about our need for spirit, a sense of belonging to and being embedded in something bigger than ourselves or our creations. We need to know that we emerged from nature and will return to it upon death. We need to have sacred places that are not just opportunities to harvest resources but are worthy of respect and veneration.

For many of us, a personal experience with the wild informs us of the existence of things that are priceless beyond economic worth. We have asked established writers with an interest in nature and social or ecological issues to share an experience that moved them or changed them in some way and that occurred in the natural world. The enthusiastic response of the outstanding writers in this collection attests to their sense that such experiences are important. These essays confirm that we are profoundly influenced and moulded by our surroundings.

The contributors to this book live in Australia, Great Britain,

Canada, and the United States, thereby providing an inadvertent comparison of perspectives from different parts of the globe. Both Australians describe dramatic, life-changing occurrences at sea. The British authors relate experiences in tamer versions of the natural world—a park, a country lane, a common. Many of the Canadian authors express explicit concern for the fate of wilderness, and several of their stories take place in the vast expanses of the Canadian landscape—the prairies, the vistas of the North—or describe the harshness and danger of northern winters. The American essays revolve around interactions with creatures of the wild—a run-in with yellow jackets, watching or following deer, fly-fishing in a spring creek. All the authors write with passion and eloquence.

I cannot omit commenting on the contribution of one author. Timothy (Tiff) Findley was one of Canada's most talented and celebrated writers. Tragically, Tiff died just as the proofs of the book came in. His partner, Bill Whitehead, informed us that this was Tiff's last piece of writing and that the subject was especially dear to his heart. It is an honour and a privilege to have his final original work to grace this book.

BETH POWNING

The Way Back Home

BETH POWNING's *writing and photography have been published in magazines and literary journals. Her first book was* Seeds of Another Summer. *Her second book, the memoir* Shadow Child, *was shortlisted for the 2000 Edna Staebler Award. She lives on a 300-acre farm near Sussex, New Brunswick, with her husband, Peter.*

I

THE WOODS OF MY CHILDHOOD were not far from the house. I could see the trees from my bed; on summer mornings the cold, exuberant tumble of birdsong broke my sleep, voices coming as if from far away and then growing steadily louder until I opened my eyes to see leaves lifting in the first breath of sunrise, passing the light back and forth like good news. I could hear the deep-bellied bawling of the neighbour's cows and a clatter of pans downstairs in the kitchen. My eyes shut and I gazed with interest at the insides of my eyelids. Red and golden speckles spun in a golden-black sea. My window was wide open and a leaf-smelling breeze stroked my cheek.

I sat up in bed. Light shone through my cotton nightgown as it had shone through my eyelids. I yawned, watching a wasp wakening on the windowsill. As the sun rayed through the treetops, the wasp raised its wings; they quivered, translucent as age-ambered parchment. I set my bare feet on the wooden floorboards, noticing that the birds had quieted, had begun, perhaps, to preen their breast feathers or drop suddenly from the branches where they had proclaimed themselves throughout the coming of the fierce light.

THERE WERE FIVE DAIRY FARMS within a half-mile radius of our house. Their lives pulsed around us, as much a part of sky and wind as peepers or summer rain. Because of them, pastures sprouted thistles; down at the pond iridescent water pooled in cow-prints; the air smelled of silage and manure and hay. Most people lived and worked at home. Women inhabited linoleum-floored kitchens or strode in fields wielding sticks. They were more sound than sight, like the hidden frogs or birds whom I knew only by their voices. The women had sour Yankee voices, German voices, one shrieking Bronx voice. They had bent fingers with dirt-encrusted nails, toad-soft floury skin, bib-aprons, and laced black shoes. Their husbands had bodies like tree trunks, spare and leaning; they smelled of grease, oil, tobacco, and their eyes glinted like breaking clouds. Tractors and manure spreaders passed below our house, which was red and stood on a bank overhung by the swaying branches of a weeping willow. Our woods were like an island, floating in a sea of stone-walled pastures and fields.

SO WHEN I WENT UP over our own horse pasture to play in the woods on this summer morning of birdsong, I was at home, like everyone else. My mother did not worry about me, since the woods had known borders that emerged in neighbours' fields; I was immune to poison ivy; the snakes were benign; and there were neither humans nor bears.

When I climbed through the broken place in the stone wall, our red house lay beneath me, cupped in the valley fields. I was up higher, in a place like the starry sky. Even though it was close and part of home, it seemed like a hidden kingdom where spirits ensured that everything was connected: clouds bent to rocks; shadows cooled lichen. Ferns shaded the tiny leaves of wild blueberries, a white cloud slid forward, and a bird made a searing cry, as if in warning. Like an unquestioned king, the sun had a path to travel and moved higher as the morning passed until, at noon, grass blades, rocky ledges, and grape leaves were shadow-doubled; and the woods lay motionless beneath its dominion.

The wind too was another being; it grew from somewhere over the western hills, came scything through the hayfields making black swaths, seized the treetops, and tousled their dignity. Or it took small breaths and then sighed through the clearing at the trees' edge, which was neither pasture nor field, where a small wind could wend its way between rock piles and red hawkweed, could release the hot spice of juniper and the resin of rotting pine needles. And stretching away around me was a community of trees whose neighbourhoods I knew: a grove of stern young maples; fey paper birches that either loved the wind or were dead, ice-bent; wicked apple trees clawed with black twigs; and by a tiny shallow pond, the benignant oak whose crown could be seen from every farmhouse in the valley, like a grandfather whose absence is unimaginable.

Here, when I was very small, I played away the summer mornings. I slid into the light and shade of the grey-skinned maples and waded waist-deep through the shadow-flecked glade, brushing my hands over feathery ferns whose tips licked the air like green tongues. One day I saw a rock covered with a shawl of green moss and squatted to stroke it—it was dense and soft, unspringy, like the matted hair of an ancient pony. Now I was in the ferns' world; I looked up and saw that the undersides of their fronds were golden and spotted with brown spores. Sturdy stems lifted a ceiling of leaves, which rocked on the air like lily pads. The light was aqueous, lilting, and I imagined myself to be four inches tall.

Or in the little clearing I sprawled on my belly in the cricketing warmth and watched the life of ants. I built houses with pebbles, roofed them with oak leaves. I scratched roads in the dirt with sticks, pretended that juniper berries were grey horses, and made their feed troughs from acorns. Mica glittered on the rock pile where water snakes sunned themselves. I squirmed closer and lay on my belly watching them. They too were intimates of this world. Glaucous hoods slid over berry-black eyes. Red tongues flickered like heat-lightning from their eternal smiles. The sun sank into the crevasses between their glossy scales, and squiggly squares patterned their coils, like turtle shells, or designs in dried mud.

And I thought that the snakes listened to a bird cry that sheered over the chirr of insects; I thought that the oak tree heard it, and the green frogs in the pond beneath its limbs. I thought that the ferns took the cry into their grass-floored halls and that it rode the lovely, rippling beds of wild violets up by the spring. The wind snatched and twisted the cry; sun glittered on the granite boulders as it died away, falling down the air. I did not understand what the bird said, but I perceived that everything else in the woods listened attentively. Thus in the knowledge that this was a community and that here was a lan-guage did I feel the first glimmer, and glamour, of life's mystery.

Because I did not understand this language and because nothing in the woods cared for me or acknowledged my presence, I was myself to myself, whole unto every moment. I loved the woods but did not call it love. I lay pressed against the earth solid as stone, shelled in drowsy heat like a pea in a pod. It was deep summer, the time of humidity and thunderstorms, of daisies and snapping turtles: the day passed into me even as I drifted unaware through time, thinking neither of the day's ending nor of its beginning.

11

VALENTINE'S DAY, 1998. My husband and I, on that day, had been married nearly thirty years. I gave him a card that said, "Just the two of us . . ." We brought our outdoor clothes from the unheated hall and lay them on the kitchen floor to warm: felt-lined boots, double mitts, neck warmers. Our farmhouse lies at the end of a valley in the Caledonian Highlands of New Brunswick. The fields glittered in the early-afternoon sunlight; it had snowed and then rained; now, on this bitterly cold day, there was a crust so thick that we could walk anywhere without breaking through.

We set out on snowshoes. They were small "cats' paws" made of aluminum with crampons that bit at every step. We crossed the lower fields, heading up to the woods, the points of our ski poles rhythmically puncturing the crust. We left behind our white farmhouse with its grey-shingled outbuildings; every field rose up the bowled hills, so no matter which direction we took, it was not long before the place we live seemed insignificant, its steel roofs a cluster of angled slants, like the bony shells of barnacles.

I was thinking of neither love nor time as we left the fields behind, following the brook whose voice we could not hear, so deeply was it buried. A wind rose; we heard a high roaring sigh that faded and then started up again, far off, and rushed towards us. The uppermost branches of the trees—ice-crowned, graced by prismatic lace—danced stiffly, creaking; shattered light spun round every twig, dazzling against the dark blue sky, and then our snowshoes crunched over tubes of ice that clattered down. I was feeling only the peaceful warmth of exertion rising from the elastic spring of toned muscles, and the pleasure of shared delight. Peter pointed with a ski pole. I looked up as a raven flew low, seemingly incurious but opening its beak just as it passed over us, making one plaintive croak; we could hear its wings spading the air like a fan with a missing blade.

The brook leads up to a ravine where cliffs rise like a ship's prow. From May until November the brook emerges from their base after a long descent between rocky walls; it tumbles down mossy chutes, splashes into pools where it spreads, black as a horse's eye; and then bends again over the lip of the next fall. There it breaks, is revealed in its separateness: flying droplets, white spume, rainbow mist. We reached the cliff and stood in the shadows, breathing the bitter air. Forty-foot spears of blue ice hung from the cliff's edge. The waterfall was frozen, although at its top we could see an opening like a window onto another world where water still sheered down, disappearing far beneath the crystal-flecked, massed meringues of ice. We could not stay here long—it was too cold—but we couldn't resist creeping into a shallow cave behind the ice columns. The ice cave forms every winter and yet we were still amazed by its presence, as fascinated by its dank snugness as we were the first time we stood at the foot of the ice-gripped ravine. We crawled in behind the hanging ice and crouched, pressed together, holding a thermos lid in mittened hands. The place felt both safe and treacherous, a hiding place without comfort, a deadly refuge. We shared a Valentine's Day cup of tea, and each other's blessed warmth.

Up on the hillsides the winter sun lay in golden trapezoids intersected by tree shadows. I led the way, shouting for Peter to follow. I loved how my crampons took me to places we did not ordinarily go, for these hills were too steep for skiing or walking. He demurred, but I persisted and so he followed. We walked straight up between the motionless trees, stamping our crampons into the ice, reaching out with our poles and stabbing the crust, stopping to pant. I had almost reached the top and could smell the spruce trees that curved down over a rockier soil. I stepped sideways. Suddenly my crampons had no purchase and I felt myself begin to slip. I lunged forward, reached for a tree. I fell, twirled on the ice. I sensed a great motion from Peter, saw him begin to fall even as he reached for me, felt myself begin to slide on my back, thought I would catch a tree, reached, and felt bark tear past my mittens.

He called my name and I heard fear. My body gathered speed; I fell too fast to reach or react; I felt helplessness like something being torn from my hands. I crashed into a tree with one shoulder, was thrown sideways, plummeted headfirst backwards at accelerating speed, unable to turn, to catch anything, to dig in my heels. I thought with amazed clarity that the next thing to hit would be the back of my neck and that I would be paralyzed or killed. My mind, like my body, had no volition, had time only to register the sense of being in the grip of a great force, a wonder that I could do nothing to help myself, and an awareness of the implacable, steel-hard resistance of this multitude of peaceful, shadow-casting trees.

Then my leg caught, my body swung hard against it, and I came to a stop and rolled forward, hanging like a taloned mouse. I heard Peter shouting. He plunged downward by lunging from tree to tree.

Something had given way in my knee. I was entangled in the branches of a bush, my leg hooked around the trunk of a young maple. Peter was beside me.

"Something's wrong with my leg."

He glanced down, his arm around a birch. We were only halfway down the hill. Not a single step could be taken without falling. The sun had reached the western hills. Cold air streamed up from the darkening valley, carrying the smell of ice.

We spoke with focused intensity, planning how we would get down. He would wedge himself against a tree, I would take his hands, I would swing loose, and he would haul me across the gap. This we accomplished, and he heaved me like a bag of grain against the tree. Thus, in slow stages, we reached the trail at the bottom. There I looped my arms over his neck and stood on the backs of his snowshoes.

When we reached the fields, the crust was flushed with the rays of the setting sun, glittering as the sun shifted, and in the hollow the apple trees of the little orchard were already crouched in blue shadow. He left me wedged in the rocks of a cairn and ran down to the house to get a toboggan. He loped awkwardly, running on snowshoes. I watched his red coat going across the field and then leaned forward with my face in my hands and felt sobs rise in me so heavy that my chest could barely lift them. This was not ordinary weeping. This grief came from the heart of February, had been quivering in the ice cave and the tea we shared there, had stretched within the golden light and the blue shadows. It rose from my soul and I could not check it. For an instant I had been like a wind-tossed bird in whose heartbeat lives the owl's talons. For an instant I had known both love and its ending.

III

MY HUSBAND, WHO IS AN artist, has his studio just across the barn-yard, so for the rest of the winter, at least, I was not alone. I sat on the edge of the dining-room table with my legs dangling and tried to lift my leg backwards but couldn't. I dragged it behind me as I took the stairs one step at a time: *step*-step, *step*-step, tipping from my hip, clutching the bannister for balance. I dreamed that I carried a cow stanchion around my neck. I studied *Gray's Anatomy*, packed bags of frozen peas around my knee. Eventually I acquired a leg brace and a surgery date: June.

Meanwhile, Peter skied, as we would have done together, but only shrugged when I asked him (jealously, wistfully) what was happening in the woods. He would only answer, "The skiing's terrible," and tell me how he had used the wrong wax or worn too many clothes as he shrugged from his coat which, as winter waned, brought the earth-sharp smell of wet ferns, granular snow, and river water into the dusty kitchen. The house had not changed. It was as it had been in the fall when we readied it for winter, with pleasure, like provisioning a boat for a long journey. Then we had been contained within the dark nights, the kitchen stove dropping coals from its grate, onion braids reflected in the glossy window, and snowdrifts like great mufflers winding round the house. Our skis leaned against the cracked plaster, Peter read out loud about Arabian deserts while I sat cross-legged, snow-tanned, knitting wool socks. The house, then, was alive and appropriate, and we loved the storms, which began with the portentous spit of ice on our windows and rose, overnight, to shrieking gales.

But in late March the light changed and revealed the passing of an epoch. Another winter's journey had been navigated. So the light announced, falling on the empty onion braid, which shed papery skin, and on a bouquet of dried hydrangeas whose petals would turn to powder if crushed. From the windows I could see the pewter rooster tail of the brook as it leaped down from the ravine, twisting through the pasture. I could see how the snow lay like diminishing islands, drifting on the brown hills. I stood on the wooden sill of the shed door watching spring shadows stretch from the eaves of the barns, listening to the voices of robins and freshets.

The accident had put an end to a time that I now remembered with yearning. I looked back at the winter when we skied every day, understanding why Inuit have dozens of words for snow, when we had seen two weasels looping through the deep drifts of the lower field, or found an entire grouse fresh-killed and surrounded by marten prints, or stood on the treeless expanse of the blueberry barrens and watched the veiled twist of crystals as snow windspiralled like tumbleweed over a prismatic desert, and had returned home to the cavelike kitchen, our mitten liners sweat-soaked, our cheeks cold-parched. I couldn't accept that they had not continued, those balanced days. I stood in the back door listening to the spring evening, whose elements I had not witnessed as they grew, vanished, arrived: the free-running brooks whose ice had broken, turned to slush, capsized as it rolled downstream; the shrill mating calls of tree frogs, pulsing from the swamp; wind softened by the red tasselled fringes of budding trees; the hollow thunder of snipes' wings. I felt excluded, not having participated in the continuum of change. And my mind swung, as it had for months, from past to future, from the time when I could walk to the time when I would walk again; and I turned from the evening birdcall, from the damp air sharp with the scent of mud and alder buds, and went to the living room, where I kept exercise pads, rolled towels, rubber stretching bands.

Every night, Peter helped me. I lay on my belly as he lifted my leg, observing minute improvements with elaborate praise. Friends telephoned. I was between drafts of a book, waiting for my editor to send comments. In this limbo, I waited for my knee surgery, and although I was surrounded with people who loved me, I felt a vague, disturbing sense that I was in the process of displacement, of loss, that I was growing dry-rooted, brittle, without resources, un-replenished, like a piece of ground dependent upon the waters of a spring.

I WOKE, AT NIGHT, FROM a recurring nightmare. The dream would begin with Peter's cry when I fell. It was the sound of a loss too great to comprehend, of pain beyond bearing, which I had forced to articu-lation by my foolishness. My body would be reduced to a wind-flung shard, a piece of anything broken from something greater: a drop of water spun from the lip of a wave, a broken twig or a wet leaf—and in the dream I would be torn and flung with accelerating speed through a dark place where there was no love, no caring, a place of absolute passionless obliviousness to my own tender filagree of self.

I flew forward, night after night, carried away from my mate, lost in darkness, where, it seemed, love had no place.

IT WAS A FEELING OF groundlessness; as once, when a child, I stepped confidently onto a muddy escarpment jutting from a river-bank only to find it to be brown froth and tumbled into the water face-first, to my brother's delight. My great-great-grandmother wrote, in letters found in an attic, of death as a "translation to the beautiful home." I dreamt of my own death, but in the dream it was in Peter's cry that I felt my home, not in the formless darkness, the "good night," where there was only terror. I found myself, that spring before my leg was fixed, sitting on the couch reading of the world's religions, wondering why I felt at home in none of them; faith, I guessed, cannot be chosen, just as I was unable to fix my knee despite my best efforts. Yet what made me heartsick was a sense that love was not enough to dispel my feelings of desolation, even though my dream told me that I should be content to rest within its embrace.

Still I grieved for the tiny signatures of spring that I was missing. I knew that the woods were not aware of my longing or affected by my absence, just as I knew that that one false step on the icy hillside might have carried me to my death and that a chickadee might have perched on the tree that broke my neck and sent its territorial challenge into the air, unaware of Peter's despair. Such things I imagined during the months in which I did not burn my Christmas wreath to mark winter's passing; did not walk in rubber boots to the pussy-willow bush by the mailbox to clip an armful of soft blossoms; did not witness the pepper of snow fleas or spiders swarming in the dead, sun-warmed grass; did not see the kildeer's nest, which the horses carefully avoided (a depression, nothing more, filled with brown-speckled eggs); did not marvel at the first flock of robins, fifty in all, Peter told me, grazing like deer on the sere hillsides.

Spring came tumbling down around us, as suddenly present as winter's absence, arriving before I had accepted the passing of the frozen nights; new life came bursting forth in all its evanescence, every bud liable to winds or the lips of deer, every egg vulnerable to predatory foxes, the soil of riverbanks torn into rivers, the wind-driven clouds dissolving and reshaping even in passage. The grass became long enough to pass shadows up a hillside. There was no hesitation; swallows claimed the eaves beneath our roofs, began importing grass and mud. And in this season nothing was more apparent than how one minute rolled into the next, or rather how what was one thing exploded into another, and there was no stillness, it seemed, anywhere.

IV

IN JUNE, I HAD MY knee surgery, and finally my leg was free to bend.
Ligaments knit and muscles gradually strengthened. I went headlong
from my forlorn end-of-winter limbo into the brief intensity of
northern summer. The books I had been studying (*The Ways of Asian
Wisdom, Religions of the World*) lay abandoned on the coffee table, since
now, like the swallows, we felt the urgency of the light-filled days,
which would last only so long. Finally, by late summer, we began the
season's harvest: I made jam and applesauce, froze broccoli and chard,
dug potatoes, pulled carrots, braided onions, bunched herbs. Peter
put aside work in his studio to replace and repair broken skylights,
rotting sills, leaky roofs. We banked the house with fir boughs gathered from the woods, tossed firewood into cellars, caulked windows,
put up storm doors. Then, when the crickets were still pulsing in the
grasses, the wild asters not yet frozen and the hillside only rusty, we
left on our annual trip to deliver Peter's glass and bronze sculptures
to galleries in Ontario and Quebec.

The night of our return, we lay in our bed under the sloping
plaster ceiling of our bedroom, the window open, and we listened,
startled, to the quiet of the country night. A branch scratched the
steel roof; then came a patter of hawthorn berries. The crickets were
silent. The brook was dry. Summer had vanished and I listened to its
absence, thinking how I had not used its loveliness to replenish
myself. All summer, it seemed, we'd planned to canoe the Saint John
River or hike the Fundy coast and then did not, choosing instead to
chase the summer's goals. And there it was again, the groundless feeling of last spring when I was housebound: I felt a longing for something so close it had no shape, a sense of ragged edges, unravelling.

SO HERE I AM, NOW, on October seventh, the day after our return, seeking the woods. I'm walking by the pond. It is warm, windy. The first of the autumnal storms is on its way up the coast, and the poplar leaves will be gone by tomorrow night. The crickets have wakened in the watery warmth; they make a dark, pulsing cry like the grating of carrots: *scrape scrape* stop—*scrape*. Be here, I say, realizing as I do so that I have been preoccupied with myself, inattentive, since the moment of my accident. *Be here.* There's a soft splash and I look up to see that a duck has flown out of the reeds, whose curved leaves flash like scimitars as the sun breaks from scudding clouds. The duck circles once, not looking down, but with urgency, as if imprinting the air with a brief, taut description of its summer grounds; then it sets off southwards with its wings flapping, and my spirits lift as I stand with my hand shading my eyes, watching until it dwindles into a speck. I go down over the meadow. In the sedgy ground along the brook, I see the soft reds and browns of dried meadowsweet on their grey stalks; of gone-to-seed goldenrod bent all in one direction; of the ribboned dried leaves clinging to steeplebush; of blackened sensitive fern, curled inwards. The dry meadow grasses stir in the warm wind and make a new sound, a sighing like sand in a box, making me think of possibilities, the sifting of priorities.

I cross the brook on steppingstones and walk along the path beneath the alders, whose leaves shine like silver blades. A raven flies over me, makes its munching gobble-cry. The raven, I know, has acknowledged me, has tipped its eye down briefly and then called a warning. What raven cry, I wonder, means *human?* Insects bob as if on strings, the blue-winged, white-bodied shiny ones that drift aimless, wind-borne, in October, harbingers of snow; and the wind, as it roams the leafless trees, makes a clean, crisp winter sound, a gathering roar like surf backwashed through pebbles just before rising to a larger wave.

I am here, now. I'm walking with my head thrown back and my eyes open. I'm back in the woods, my legs swinging at the knee, my boots landing softly on moss, or snapping twigs.

I enter a grove of poplars. The ground is matted with a tapestry of round leaves. Some are black, stippled with green spots; some are gold with brown speckles or brown with black patches. I brush knee-deep through hay-scented fern. Red leaves lie belly-up, their dried points stiff and pointed inward like the paws of dead squirrels. I come out in a large clearing filled with red bunchberry leaves. The air smells of dried ferns, bark, spruce resin, leaf stems; it is a slow, ancient scent, sweet and tangy as simmering apples, both savage and sleepy.

I reach the brook. I clamber down its bank and sit on a rock with my back against wrist-thick spruce roots. Leaves spiral on the air, tap against the water, which folds in black rills wherever it is interrupted by stone or boulder. There are fish the size of dagger blades. They flick beneath boulders, where I can see their snouts, waiting.

And like the fish, I too wait. I lean back. My eyes swing with the water: downstream, up again. Downstream, up again. And the leaves float down over the little fall and build up against a stick, one by one by one. Like the pages of a book. Water-riffled. The water, viscous as oil where the leaves rest. And a bird calls, once.

IS THIS FAITH? FOR I believe there is spirit, here. They are here, the spirits of my childhood woods. Or is it one spirit? One voice?

The woods are still. Most of its birds have left; no blossoms reach for light; there is no soft-leaved wind-dance. This quiet is the preamble to winter's frozen crouch; but in the stillness I sense spring, even though it is hidden: shrouded queen bees, gall-coiled larvae, folded stalks of fern, scale-covered buds, nested mice beneath stumps, beetle eggs in bark tunnels, stoneflies beneath river rocks. Nothing is finished; no death has been without its beginning. Soil-clung seeds lie in bone-rich soil, and the great horned owl clings to a branch somewhere near the tamaracks with his head swivelled backwards, eyes hooded, waiting for dusk.

There is no love here. Yet should I hear the low hoot of the owl (as we did, once, Peter and I, sitting together on the hillside at dusk watching the moon-sliver, followed by a lower voice answering the first; back and forth they went, clearly responding, one owl to the other across the darkening trees), my heart would be lifted; something would open inside me, joy entering as I'm moved by my own love for this wild, passionless beauty.

I am not the child who lay on her stomach watching the drowsy snakes; that little girl basked in childhood's timelessness and had no fear of endings. Snakelike, she coiled round the day's heart and heard its voice. "And the mystery," Dylan Thomas wrote, "sang alive . . ." No, I am older and growing old, and as my own time dwindles I love more fiercely and yet feel love's restless anguish. So I put my head back against this tree, which moves gently, not breathing but alive; there is either one voice or so many voices they are countless. Every instant becomes one, and every voice is gathered. My fingers reach and touch wet stones. I may spend the rest of my life finding my way back home.

BILL McKIBBEN

A Desperate Clarity

BILL McKIBBEN *is the author of* The End of Nature, *the first book for a general audience about global warming, now in twenty languages. He has written six other books, and his work also appears in the* New York Times, *the* New Yorker, Harper's, *the* Atlantic, Outside, *and many other national publications. He is currently a visiting scholar at Middlebury College.*

I REMEMBER ONCE HIKING with my friend the naturalist and writer Terry Tempest Williams. We were near my home in the Adirondack Mountains of upstate New York, working our way up a steep, piny trail, when all of a sudden she came to a halt and dropped to her knees. There in front of her was a newt in its red eft phase—maybe three inches long, neon orange.

Now these newts are, at various seasons and in various places, nearly ubiquitous—I've counted them by the hundreds on mile-long portages to small ponds; I've shamelessly used them as enticements to keep my daughter going on trails; I've even stopped and admired their bulbous architecture and articulated gait. So it was fun to sit with Terry for a moment and show off my measly store of natural history lore.

For a moment. Even five moments. But right about then I started to get a little bored. And started to realize, not for the first time, what a miserable excuse for a nature lover I was. Terry could—and did—crouch there on her haunches for a good half hour, lost in the world of the newt. It was enough to fill her imagination—a world in a grain or two of orange amphibian. Some people—and surely once upon a time most people—just connect to the world around them, easily and profoundly.

But I—well, I was bored. I wanted to push on to the top. That was our goal, after all. Motion. This incident reminded me how little I really was in contact with the outdoors despite all the thousands of hours I spend there each year. Mostly I float along in a self-contained bubble of my own thoughts, plans, and hopes, my mind firing away like a pinball machine, each new thought a flashing light or ringing bell to distract me from the reality at hand. I can walk a mile or two at a speedy clip and realize that I've hardly seen anything, that I'm in almost as deep a glaze as when I'm driving. I'll stop for a moment when I get to the top of a hill or a mountain—the big picture will move me—but then it's on and on. I'm outside but I'm inside.

The moments when that sac is punctured and the world comes flooding in are sweet—they linger in my memory, the moments I will savour someday when I'm down to my last few hours. Some of them are dramatic—full moon rising while I'm on a glacier high on Mount Rainier, the light revealing the curve of the earth. Some are subtle—three or four days into a solo backpacking trip, when I suddenly realize that the little newscaster who lives in my head has temporarily run short of things to say and has simply shut up. But none was more profound than the day when they almost got me.

"They," in this case, does not mean grizzly bears or mountain lions or tiger sharks. The Adirondacks, for all its millions of acres of big wilderness, is a pretty tame place. No poisonous snakes, save for one colony of timber rattlers along Lake George. No nasty carnivores. Wolves exist only in hopeful rumour; the panther was extirpated. There's hardly even any poison ivy. You can get giardiasis, but that's about it.

Or so I thought until, walking in the woods behind my house, I stepped on a yellow jacket nest. I was hiking off trail, a couple of miles from home, dog at my side. As usual, I was deep in some extremely important line of thought, probably having to do with an enormously wise piece of writing I was about to undertake. And then, all of a sudden, there was the most unbelievable pain washing up my stomach toward my neck. It came so fast, as pure a splash of feeling as if someone had tossed a pot of boiling water in my direction. And it hurt so much, a purity of pain I've never experienced before or since. In my memory it expresses itself almost as a flash of white light.

At first I had no idea what was going on. I was climbing a very steep slope, which is why the yellow jackets were at waist level when they boiled out of the hill. I couldn't see them—I just turned and ran, which is hard on a 40-degree incline. I hadn't gone five steps before I cracked into a tree branch, cutting my forehead and closing one eye. But the pain was still there, and with nothing to fight, my flight reflex kept pumping. Finally, after a quarter mile of nearly blind flight, just a few insects were still clinging to me and I was able to pull off my shirt and flick them off.

The pain subsided from a shriek to a roar. I collected enough of my wits to get started home (thankful for all the thousands of hours I'd spent wandering that forest so that the landmarks were obvious even to my frazzled mind). But I hadn't gone very far before hives started to appear across my torso—big, swelling cones. I am cursed with an overactive imagination, and I instantly began to recall stories I'd heard of people dying from bee stings—how their throats swelled shut and they choked to death, unless there was someone standing by with a scout knife ready to perform an emergency tracheotomy. My dog was the best dog I've ever had, but I doubted she was up to surgery. Statistics started flashing in my brain: how often had people downplayed some danger (avalanche, lightning, shark attack) by saying, "More people die each year of bee stings"? It's a very comforting thought, until you step on a yellow jacket nest.

That panic gave way, though, to the most remarkable set of emotions I can recall. Suddenly I found myself praying, and it was not the prayer you might expect. Instead it was a psalm of thanks: Thank you, God, for this hemlock stand, in all its drooping hemlockness. Thank you, God, for that old yellow birch snag, rotting where it leans, ventilated with sapsucker holes. Thank you for that crow, for those wintergreen shrubs, for that living, sparkling creek, for the humidity, the damp, hanging air. Thank you for gravity, which I seemed to feel as a force for the first time. I stopped a second to stroke the bark of a red pine, all jigsaw rough. I didn't see a red eft, but there was a small pile of deer droppings, a drift of blue feathers where a bird had met its end, a vein of quartz in a grey rock. Any such sight could have occupied me for hours—it was as if I were part of all this, not some observer or, worse yet, some astronaut wandering through it sustained by the oxygen of his chattering thoughts. The boundaries had blurred.

The high didn't last, of course. Within half an hour I was home, and my wife was screaming at the blood pouring down my face, and I was screaming at her to forget about the goddamn blood and get me to the hospital. Which is a long way away from where we live— by the time we arrived, the hives were so spectacular that the doctor stretched me out on a gurney and started sticking ivs into my wrists. Before long there were steroids and antihistamines and all manner of stuff flowing in, and some hours later I was back home and had the radio on and the newspaper in my face, and all was back to normal.

But not completely back to normal. It was as if the tears of pain had irrigated my eyes, and for weeks afterward the world seemed in sharper focus whenever I stepped outside. Have you ever had a brand-new car, with a perfectly clean windshield? Or cleaned a pair of really grimy eyeglasses? It was like that, except emotionally. Everything seemed dear and noble and complete. I seemed to move in the world, not through it. The layers of insulation between me and the real world had been removed, and now the breeze was whistling through. You could say this new state had a dreamlike quality, but it would have been more accurate to say just the opposite—that it felt as if I had woken up from a dream.

Slowly, of course, I've fallen back asleep. The newscast inside my head has returned to full volume, or nearly so. As maybe it has to— I'd go crazy, or write poetry, if I were that open to the world all the time. The flood of sensation, and of a kind of love, was very nearly unbearable in its beauty. And yet I desperately want it back too—and wonder if it really takes an experience of finding yourself lower down on the food chain for it to kick in. Is it human nature that abstracts us from the world, or is it some effect of consumer culture? Can we be creatures too, and find some of our satisfaction there—or are we condemned to keep the world forever at arm's length? That's a deeper question than I'm qualified to answer—the best stab at it I've ever read is in David Abram's book *The Spell of the Sensuous*—but it seems to me one of the key questions that we face.

And here is how I'd like to pose it. We speak often, and sentimentally, of being "enchanted" by the natural world. But what if it's the other way around? What if we are enchanted, literally, by the human world we live in? That seems entirely more likely—that the consumer world amounts to a kind of lulling spell, chanted tunefully and eternally by the TV, the billboard, the suburb. A spell that convinces us that the things we want most from the world are comfort, convenience, security. A spell that by now we sing to each other. A spell that, should it start to weaken, we try to strengthen with medication, with consumption, with noise. A slightly frantic enchantment, one that has to get louder all the time to block out the troubling question constantly forming in the back of our minds: "Is this all there is?"

If so, then as individuals and as a society the deep question becomes how to break that spell. A kiss offers the traditional antidote, of course, but a kiss is what the culture keeps giving us. A nice, soft kiss, day after day. Sometimes a shirt full of bees seems more effective. "Turn off the air conditioner," the great desert writer Ed Abbey would tell tourists when he was a ranger at Arches National Monument in southwest Utah. "Take off your sunglasses. Get out of the car." Feel the heat, feel the cold, feel *something*. All those senses—all those emotions—work outside the narrow range in which we normally set our personal thermostats.

It is a sorry thing to admit that you're so thick it takes seventy-six yellow jacket bites to pierce you. I hope I never get a booster shot; I want to learn how to do it with newts too. But the lesson was well worth the price—that desperate clarity was one of the greatest gifts the world ever gave me. When I try to imagine the holy spirit, I hear buzzing.

DAVID ADAMS RICHARDS

Land

DAVID ADAMS RICHARDS *was born in Newcastle, New Brunswick, and for the last five years has lived in Toronto with his family. He is the author of numerous books of fiction and nonfiction and is the recipient of many awards, including the 1985 Governor General's Award for* Nights Below Station Street *and, most recently, the Giller Prize for his novel* Mercy Among the Children.

I

THE HOUSE WAS OWNED by my friend's uncle—a white house with a small, enclosed veranda, where a faded, flowered swing listed to the southwest, while autumn sun glinted on six window panes. The uncle used to drink Napoleon wine there on sunny days, watching the bird feeders he had placed on the maple trees, and sometimes picking off the squirrels if too many of them started chasing away the birds.

A host of crab trees, gnarled from the roots up, grew haphazardly in the back, in a field of yellow grass, where the deer came out. At the end of this field sat a barn with a sagging roof, where a horse of little worth had lived out its life. Uncle Tate, a widower, fed it and kept it warm but used it for nothing and cursed it in the pasture.

A veteran of the Second World War, he died in 1963, cutting a new road through for the Frazer Lumber mill. I remember Alden Nowlan's answer to "A little hard work never killed anyone":

"My God—hard work kills people all the time."

It is what those who have not worked, or known those who have, have forgotten.

There was no one to take his house. A distant cousin said it was his. A sister of that cousin said it was hers. I forget how things finally transpired; land was argued over (winter trees frigid under the moon, and everyone arguing over whose moon it was).

Finally, his nephews went into the house and closed it up. What was valued was siphoned off. As teens we passed it a number of times going into the future. The nineteen-foot dory that Uncle Tate had used for herring was left high against the barn, the pathway he took to the ice field to lay out smelt nets no longer in evidence.

The Beatles came. Everyone was in love. Vietnam and love.

Neil Young sang about a place in North Ontario. Suddenly half my generation wanted to be old—or from a previous generation—a generation that did things by hand, and by rout, a generation that lived off the land, never knowing that even the First Nations them-selves wanted at least in part to escape from this. Those who had never mashed more than potatoes were talking to me about milling flour. To dispossessed youth in the cities, it was a great and risky adventure—going off to the boonies, some with their daddy's credit card, and without his blessing. Here in northern New Brunswick was one place those who wanted to change their lives came to.

So in 1972, a new Walden was to be shaped out of Uncle Tate's farmyard, his fourteen acres that bordered the bay, where the wind was so cold even by late August it could chill your blood.

The group was made up mostly of expatriate Americans, and some Canadians, and one or two from New Brunswick. One of Uncle Tate's nephews had left the farm; no longer respecting his loved ones who had shovelled shit to keep him alive, he reached out to gurus who knew far less than his father, and joined the very farm Uncle Tate had worked a little over a decade before.

2

HER NAME WAS STEVIE—she was nineteen, wore granny glasses, and knitted in Uncle Tate's kitchen as the sunlight glanced over the chimes. She was from Toronto, and the fellow, her mentor, and the mentor of the group, Darren, came from New York. I have a memory of him looking like Jesus, leaning against Uncle Tate's sink and pouring water out, as if at a baptismal:

"Man, you guys don't know what you have—paradise—so you'd better take care of it," he said, pouring out his cup of clear well water. That is, he ordered me to take care of something his own urban culture had reduced to nothing.

"We got a lot a winter," I said.

"That's cool," he said. "That's cool—just get yerself an old lady and tuck in."

"What was your uncle like?" she asked my friend. "Was he a fine man?"

My friend turned beet-red.

"He was a sawed-off five-foot-five-inch redneck," my friend said, "who got into fights."

They both laughed, and he looked pleased.

"He was a fine man," I whispered in apology, not to them—but to Uncle Tate for the utter weakness of his nephew.

Tate was a fine man. But not the way they were thinking. When he came back to New Brunswick from the Second War, he was as wild as a buck and as rough as a night in jail. Peace and love he had in abundance but not the kind to suffer fools. He'd walk across the river in late March, with the ice breaking around his boots, to get to a dance. That was faith. He was completely colourblind; he'd love and hate indiscriminately. He got into a fight with the doctor and was in jail when his wife died alone. He never forgave himself that.

By the questions they asked about his life I knew they were hoping for a working-class hero, not hoping for a man, but someone they had seen in some movie. And his nephew from rural New Brunswick was so ashamed of his heritage he wanted to belittle it in front of his betters so he could belong—belong to those who wanted to churn butter to prove they were morally superior to a man now dead, who at five foot five was as strong as a bull.

I don't think I ever cared for his nephew after this day.

3

I DISCOVERED FROM THIS NEPHEW that the newcomers had not come here to learn from the Whites anyway; they did not want what the Uncle Tates knew, but to study the First Nations, to learn from them. There would be no going back to what they had all come from. But the First Nations by now owned cars, high-powered boats, TVs, and Ski-Doos, and they didn't want to go back either.

"No, there is no going back for them," my friend said happily. "They are committed to here—this place will be their roots."

"Well, then, they will need three hundred years," I said.

The older man in the group, Darren, worried about the First Nations people here.

"We've destroyed them," he said.

"Not entirely," I said (not in defence of us but in defence of them—but he did not get this subtlety).

"It's terrible the way they are treated," he continued. "The Aboriginals are caretakers of our earth—aren't they?"

No one could say Darren was wrong about the first part of the statement. I think he was scolding us with the second. Well, who in North America doesn't deserve to be scolded, more than once, about the First Nations people?

I began to realize that Darren believed in his ability not so much to belong with the First Nations, who would allow him the benefit of vicarious suffering, but to escape who he was, a white, urban, university-educated man in a denim suit with long hair and love beads. And Tate's nephew gave up his own hard-earned, blow-by-blow knowledge of life here for a notional knowledge in order to belong to a group he considered superior to those people who had already fashioned a complete life out of the soil.

In a certain respect, he was like the First Nations people who were to give up their own knowledge of life and land because the new white settlers had told them to.

Soon they were going to make a canoe of bark, fish in the traditional way, plant under the June moon—they had a pocketful of seeds. Pocketful of dreams.

4

THEY SPENT OCTOBER in the yellow trees, cutting and limbing the wood they were to burn, but didn't get it yarded until late and then left it where it was until well after the first storm. After a time they reminded me of a little band of orphans, nowhere much to go. Stevie's cheeks were often streaked with red, as if she had just cried. I wondered where she had come from. But she was here now and under orders from a guru who probably gave orders as relentlessly as any daddy she had run from. I saw her trying to carry wood to the house and stumbling under the weight, as if she were carrying a cross she could neither bear nor understand. It might have been like forcing an Indian woman to go to church in the eighteenth century. The feeling of being displaced must have been almost as great.

But she continued to carry her wood.

Watching her in those days, I thought of a thousand women who had done the same a century before—of my mother-in-law, left a widow with nine children at the age of forty-two, a country girl—of my mother, who grew up in the heart of what any one of these people would consider the wilderness and did housework from the time she was four. Of my uncle, who at thirteen was sent through the woods to find my grandfather, while my grandmother, holding a double-barrelled shotgun, held off a group who was trying to take the property. She would have shot them if she had to. For her to wax eloquent about the danger of guns and the need to take safety courses was not an option at that moment. Or of my paternal grandmother, who knocked a cow cold with one punch (a feat not to be equalled by any literary figure in Canada, save Malcolm Lowry).

When it became very cold, Stevie would sit in our corner store for hours, pretending to do crossword puzzles in the daily newspapers. She was hiding from the guru who intimidated her and intellectually bullied her.

I often saw a look of dull confusion, as if she were a lost Girl Scout. In a way her plight was a lesson to me about the First Nations, about how their lives were so finally and tragically changed after 1605. Stevie suddenly brought that home, without her ever knowing it. And where, I thought, could she ever go now? Nowhere. Not with winter setting in and no tickets home. There was a hush over the land that they had rented, and frost clung to the turned-down and twisted grasses; their wood lay yarded as haphazardly as fallen soldiers. There was no way to dispel the cold and no way to get rid of the smoke from their damp maple and birch. No way to make the light stay when it was getting dark, no way to make the chickens look happy, no way to make the barn stand straight again. No one had money for those things. And night—night came at six, at five, at four-thirty.

5

THE LOCALS BECAME INTERESTED in helping out. For no better reason (and a damn good reason it was) than these were people and it was Christmas. And many of my friends who were their age dropped in on them with presents.

They brought deer meat and homemade wine, fresh-grown grass, and other forms of libation. But it became a strange celebration. It reminded me of Tolstoy's quip that at least as much is known in the country as the city, and probably more.

When Darren spoke to us of wanting to build a geodesic dome, he was very surprised to find out that our friend Giles had quit school in grade 10 and had built the first dome in New Brunswick, drawing on his own plans and intelligence, and reading Buckminster Fuller.

When Darren said he would fish for his food, it was Peter who brought them ten smoked salmon. This was not one-upmanship. The little town was just the land extended. Until I was twenty-four, I could carry my rifle from my house into the woods for a deer hunt. It is not that Darren did not know the land—he did not know himself, and the land simply told him this. Sooner or later the land does. I know he wanted to live in harmony like the first people and wanted the First Nations people to be his champions of the forest and his protectors of the environment. But that said only one thing: he had never allowed them an option; in his life he never really looked upon them the way they should have been looked upon from the first: as men.

6

LIFE WENT ON. THERE WERE chores to be done, by people who
had never done chores before. They spoke of sharing, but it was con-
tractual, not emotional. It seemed to me there was more love in the
place when Uncle Tate lived alone and fired off his shotgun at his
visitors as a joke.

By January there were dissenters. That month a young man got
a job in town. Another went away—and then another. Tate's nephew
left in a dispute over something.

I met Stevie coming out along the back road one day. She was
carrying a saucepan, with nothing in it. Someone had told her there
were winter berries to collect, but she had found none, for there were
none. We stood and talked for a moment in the freezing gale of late
afternoon.

"We are going to have a really fine farm," she told me. I knew that
was nonsense. But I was so sorry for her at that moment. She had
come to womanhood in what kind of city, to feel so left out, like so
many of my generation? Cast out, of something. I'm not even sure
what anymore. All she had known was concrete. Why had this happened? What sad turning away from her family did she have, in what
hot, vacant urban apartment or house tucked between two asphalt
roads? An argument over the war—or a parent trying too hard to
buy her love, or loving her too little? Did they even know where she
was anymore? She was still a child really.

"So you aren't going home?" I said.

"Oh—no—no," she smiled. "I'll never go."

It was a victory for her to say this. I might have told her that I
knew a family who arrived at this little place she was now in 1840—
and lived their first winter in a cave about a mile from where we were

talking, losing three children. I might have told her my relatives came over after the battle of Culloden, and one walked from Pennsylvania in 1805 and settled up on the Norwest. To keep her chin up.

I discovered at that moment that there is something about the land—you look unnatural on it if you are unnatural, you look greedy upon it if you are, lazy if you tend to be. If you are frightened of guns or wildlife, the land will inform you. Nervous on the water, the water will let you know. There is no escaping who you are once you are here, on the Miramichi—or anywhere else, for that matter. It is what the First Nations saw of us—it is what I saw of her; she with the saucepan with nothing in it.

The man Darren who made the rules was simply selfish—and in a sense, beyond all his ethical talk of First Nations, a prude. This is what the land said he was. And the land does not lie.

7

IN LATE JANUARY ONE OF them went and got a job. He worked at a garage in Barryville repairing snowmobiles and would come home every night late. He supported this little family of outcasts by doing a job hundreds of men did without complaint simply because life required that he do it. And it was he who got to meet the First Nations on even terms, because he worked alongside the Micmac man, Jacob Paul, who co-owned the garage that repaired small engines.

Then he found a girl in Neguac and moved out.

So there was only Stevie and her mentor, Darren, left. They were the last. And in that winter, living alone, they found the dream had somehow disappeared. But what dream was it? I don't think any of them, including Darren, really knew.

Still, in some way, it must have been a noble dream, a kind of idealism that can only be hatched in torment, from a society writhing in pain. The looking for a better world, in Uncle Tate's few acres at the edge of the earth. A little society in the wilderness, born in the city, believing animals were Bambis and berries were for the taking, flying back home on a jet plane where if lucky they could still believe those things. They found here only the pain they believed they had left behind and in the end blamed us because we had no balm or magic to help them relinquish this pain. The simple pain of being women and men, no matter what land you stood on and of what race you were.

Darren left one afternoon, saying he would be back—that he was going into town for supplies. His poncho on a hook in the corner near his leather hat assured Stevie of his return. But he did not come back. She waited by the window, his supper in the warming oven. He became safe again, when being unsafe was no longer a game.

Stevie stayed by herself, looking out those porch windows, waiting for her friend. She made it until March. Sometime about St. Patrick's Day I saw her doing her crossword in the corner store. There was a storm outside and everything in the world was white.

She was happy, she said, the wood was drier, and people had made her welcome. She was working two nights a week in this store, selling cigarettes and Tampax. But she needed to take a course, she thought—and come back next year. Next year would be better. The terrible things in the world would be gone. She would get a horse, maybe one of those Morgans. Suddenly she reached up and kissed my forehead and squeezed my hand. She walked on and I watched her go out of my life. It's been almost thirty years. The house is gone, and no one waits, and none of them have ever been back. They didn't have much luck. For a while many of us might have believed a new world would come. Perhaps that's what we've all been watching for, whenever we look up at the sky.

8

I WALKED BEYOND UNCLE TATE's land last autumn. There had been two days of snow. I walked toward the hundredth new chop-down that has come since the mill started its new process. I carried my little Winchester 30:30—but I have not fired a rifle in years. I trick myself into hunting by not hunting now. Usually I find a tin can to fire at, sight the rifle in, for next year.

My family—here for over two and a half centuries—is gone from the river, and in the summer the brooks babble to tell me so. My mother died in 1978, my father died two years ago, and all the children have left. We have gone away, but we do come back. In a sense, once a part of the land, we can never leave. We didn't become peace lovers, but we do love, fiercely, I suppose.

There is no town here now. A city sprawls with lights toward its destiny. The trees are muted and thrashed, as pockets of the forest no longer exist at all.

I walked toward the high ground beyond his house, next to the power lines. The ground was dug up that day, with fresh tracks and scrapes. In one of those tricks of fate I saw the old saucepan Stevie had used to collect her winter berries. It had been tossed up out of the dirt that had buried it for years. I wondered how her life had gone, and if she had ever found the place she wanted.

Then turning toward the chop, I saw a little doe. As I approached she made a heroic attempt to stand. Her left hind leg was caught in a coyote snare, and she was hunkered down beneath the snow and thrashed trees. All around and everywhere I looked the snow and earth had been torn up, where a gigantic battle had raged above Uncle Tate's old farmyard. The night before the buck had stayed, to protect the doe in the snare from the coyotes. And he must have fought like hell. The coyotes—here almost as big as wolves—hadn't been able to get to her. I do not know if the buck lived, but he had done the job given him. Like Uncle Tate with his wife, he didn't know why she was caught up. The world had betrayed them both: the snare cynically said neither of them mattered. Still the buck had fought like a bastard. Never left his poncho on a nail.

I managed to cut the snare. She stood and bolted, cracking the limbs of some birch trees, and was gone, into what was left of a world that didn't exist any longer.

ROBERT DREWE

The Requiem Shark

ROBERT DREWE *is the author of five novels, including*
The Savage Crows *and* The Drowner, *which won numerous*
prizes, including the Book of the Year Prize. He has also
published two collections of short stories, including the Australian
classic The Bodysurfers, *and a prize-winning memoir,*
The Shark Net. *His fiction has been adapted for film,*
television, radio, and theatre. He lives with his family
on the central coast of New South Wales.

EVERY WRITER KNOWS that although coincidence may be Fiction's dire enemy, it is Real Life's ardent lover. If I didn't know this the summer I turned nineteen, I certainly understood that news editors adored the poignant coincidence.

One Sunday morning that summer I was following sharks up the West Coast Highway, well outside my territory, with the two-way radio crackling in the office Ford Anglia and the sun glinting off the white dunes and sandy verges, off the roadside bottles and approaching car windscreens and the glassy Indian Ocean itself.

Along the way I kept the news editor informed of my progress. I called him from City Beach and Scarborough and a couple of stops in between. He didn't remind me that my territory stopped at Cottesloe. He appreciated reporters sticking to a story.

"Tiger sharks," I said knowledgeably. I tried to keep the self-consciousness out of my voice when I said, "Come in!" and "Over and out!" Then I stomped through the pigface and sandhills, training the office binoculars on the unbroken sea just beyond the surf line. Where were they?

On the western horizon, as usual, Rottnest Island was mysteriously transformed by summer's atmospheric conditions into a misty string of mirage-islands. They hovered like spacecraft above the ocean, well south of the island's real whereabouts. As I searched for dorsal fins in the rise of each breaking wave, for those sinister, thrilling shadows in the swells, glistening women smelling of coconut oil glanced drowsily up at me from their beach towels. Children squinted into the glare to see what this fully clothed boy was peering at. Languid adults' faces said: What do you think you're doing?

Willing you to be eaten. The sooner the better. Well, not a kid, but definitely a well-known businessman or a sun-dried old socialite. If possible, the shark should be a rare species of record size. And I needed a garrulous old-timer as a witness. Someone like Ted "Sharky" Nelson, every reporter's favourite contact for shark stories. ("It rushed at him like a Metro bus, bit him in halves, and swallowed him in two bites. Never seen one that big this far north. Poor bastard never had a chance. I'll never forget the look on his face.")

In the best possible news world there would be still more. And not just that this excellent tragic day (Black Sunday? Bloody Sunday?) was the victim's birthday or golden wedding anniversary or that he'd just won the lottery. (Although the news editor would welcome any one of these tragic coincidences.) I wanted more than to break news. I wanted to be the news.

My fantasy front-page lead—shark attack or boating disaster or freak rip tide—was a watery adventure story where I became the hero and got the scoop as well. Naturally it would take unusual circumstances for me to step outside the traditional role of neutral observer and modestly but heroically intrude. (Frantic lifeguard, through loud-hailer: "There's still a little girl on a floatie out there! All my guys have major arterial bleeding. Does anyone on the beach have their bronze medal for lifesaving?" Me: "Well, if there's a kid's life at stake . . .")

Just as my dream scoop required loss of life (the aforementioned businessman or socialite), it required me to save lives too. And, importantly, to risk my own. Then, dripping water, and perhaps a little blood (enough for the photograph) over the Anglia's dashboard, shrugging off medical attention, and modestly keeping news of my own heroism until the fourth or fifth paragraph, I'd dictate the story over the two-way for the first edition.

In the Fremantle branch office of the *West Australian*, on the corner of Adelaide and Queen Streets, the reporting staff of two senior and two junior reporters worked out of a back room behind the classified advertisements counter and the ad salesman's and ad typist's tearoom. If anything newsworthy happened in or around Western Australia's major port, the first port of call for shipping from Europe, Asia, and Africa, we were the people who reported it.

The other junior reporter's name was John Dare—in my mind the perfect byline for an intrepid journalist. Each afternoon either Dare or I prized the daily shipping list from the reluctant sausage fingers of the harbourmaster, Captain Oliphant, whose phobia (the waterfront equivalent of worrying whether he'd left the gas on) was checking and rechecking the sailing times in case four hundred passengers missed the *Fairstar* to England. Then, in the two hours where our day and night shifts crossed and the late-afternoon sun made our shared desk uninhabitable, Dare and I played office cricket in the back corridor, with a ruler for a bat and a ball made of copy paper and Scotch tape, and cheerfully pondered ways to scoop each other.

A good fellow and a Fremantle boy himself, Dare had the advantage of local knowledge and an easier way with the cops. My own relations with the port's police hadn't recovered from my story about the retiring Fremantle police inspector whose car, accelerating away from his boozy farewell party, had mounted the pavement and struck a small girl. The paper had spiked my story, the police commissioner had denied it, and I had been characterized by the police as a troublemaker and boat rocker.

Now I needed my big coastal scoop more than ever. My hunger for it easily matched Dare's amiable street wisdom and cop-friendly banter. I even thought about the story on my own time, jogging along the beach each morning and willing a passing container ship or cray-fish boat onto the reef. I wanted the story so badly that I *studied* for it.

I went up to Perth on my days off, and in the *West Australian's* library I took out all the files on shark attacks and shipwrecks and coastal disasters since the colony's first settlement. Back at the Fremantle City Library I read up on local history too, right back to the early Dutch mariners, the Dutch East India Company, the bloody mutinies and marooned sailors. The more marine mayhem, the better.

There were tragedies I'd never heard of. Like Charles Robertson being taken by a whaler shark near the Claremont Jetty in 1923. He was a thirteen-year-old coxswain thrown laughing into the river by the crew of his Scotch College rowing shell—straight into the shark's mouth. There was the bookmaker's clerk, Simeon Ettelson, who died after a twelve-foot tiger shark mauled his thigh down to the femur in the shallows at Cottesloe in 1925. Even though they were ancient tragedies, I was surprised I'd never heard of them. I'd swum heedlessly in those places for years. Maybe those stories had been regarded as bad for the real estate market. Or maybe they'd sim-ply passed out of community memory.

Although I appreciated this sort of grisly information, I had no idea what to do with it. In the way that John Dare's Fremantle background helped him better understand the port, I wanted all this coastal knowledge to give me a background of my own. I'd spent my childhood and adolescence on the west coast's sandy moonscape, and I was sure I had something to say about it. Perhaps it could help me make sense of recent dramatic events in my own life: in short order I had become a teenage father and husband, and my mother had dropped dead of a stroke the day after seeing the baby for the first time.

For a year after her death my father lost himself in work. In the evenings he came home late, brushed my little sister's hair in front of the television, then drank Dewar's until after midnight. But by day he seemed fired with energy. He worked so hard for Dunlop Rubber that he produced the company's best sales figures for the year and won a holiday in Singapore.

He brought back duty-free gifts. Mine was an Olivetti *Lettera* portable typewriter. It was the best present he'd ever given me. The newspaper's typewriters I used every day, the industrial-strength, cigarette-burned Siemens machines chained to their wheeled metal stands, were tools of the trade, as useful and as mundane as a telephone or a desk. What those heavy-duty models plodded through— their punctuation marks and lowercase *e*'s and *o*'s punching holes through the copy paper—was work. What the little sea-green Olivetti began to produce at home was everything else.

The Olivetti started tapping out magazine stories of shark attacks and Dutch shipwrecks and mutinies along this very coast. I sent them off to barbershop magazines like the *Australasian Post* and *Weekend* and *People*. The *Australasian Post* in particular liked shark attacks, and it liked the maulings to be described in gruesome detail. For badly needed extra money, I was happy to oblige.

With my first writing cheque from the *Australasian Post*, I took my new wife, Ruth, to dinner at the Sea Crest, on Cottesloe Beach. The high tide lapped on the sand below us as we ate Steak Diane and drank Porphry Pearl and watched the sun sink like a red whale into the horizon. We were commenting favourably on the glorious sunset and behaving like sophisticated restaurant patrons when it suddenly occurred to me that our meal had been paid for by the unfortunate Simeon Ettelson, mauled by the tiger shark just below our table.

I looked down at the inoffensive waves breaking on the soft sand below and raised my glass to Mr. Ettelson. I began this small toast feeling amused at the coincidence, but by the time I put my glass down I felt unsteady and quite moved. Almost misty. As I headed to the Gents to splash water on my face, I wondered if it could be the Porphry Pearl. A minute later, I knew it was. I hadn't drunk wine before. I was a father, a husband, and a news shark, but I was still two years off the legal drinking age.

EVERYONE I KNEW LIVED NEAR the ocean shore or the wide estuary of the Swan River, which twisted and narrowed before flowing into the sea at Fremantle. Some of my friends came from families who'd been boatbuilders for four generations. Two brothers, Kimberley and Richie Male, even came from a pearling family that operated luggers in the far northwest. They'd been sent south to school, where Richie and I had been on the swimming team together.

As kids, my friends and I had crabbed and prawned and fished, patrolled the rock pools and limestone reefs with our *gidgies* and *kylies*, ten-year-old white boys' versions of Aboriginal fish spears and boomerangs. We grew up knowing the tides and reefs, the hot easterlies and blustery westerlies of the West Australian coast. We swam in competitions at the Crawley and Claremont baths, earned our life-saving bronze medallions, skin-dived, paddled canoes, built rafts, rowed boats, and crewed on ancient varnished Gwen-12s and vJs and fourteen-footers. I'd even rescued a couple of swimmers in trouble in the surf—one of them a sportswriter who later was so embarrassed that he never spoke to me again.

Despite all this coastal experience, I'd never seen a man-eating shark in its natural habitat. Nor had my friends. All we'd seen were potential man-*hurters*, plenty of them, but nothing big enough to devour us, even if they wanted to. Of course, every summer there were "sightings" of man-eaters reported in the papers. But never by anyone I knew, and never taken too seriously.

So why did I think of man-eating sharks every time I dove into the sea? It had to be that sharks were buried deep in my collective unconscious. I'd read this somewhere in my research, and I believed it. Clearly some of us were born with a fear of sharks—like the chicken's instinct for the shadow of the hawk. It was amazing what I saw in the back-froth of a snapping wave, in the darker patchwork ripples of weed and reef. Was that surge just a diving cormorant? Was the shadow really a passing cloud—or the first and last hint of the white pointer's charge? This, I thought, was obviously the under-lying anxiety of my life.

THE DAY BEFORE MY SHARK HUNT had been a blustery Satur-day in mid-November. I was bodysurfing with Richie Male and three other fellows at North Cottesloe. Richie was seventeen, a joker, an easygoing boy two years younger than I. He was in especially good spirits that afternoon because his final school examinations had finished the day before.

The southwesterly was chopping up the beach surf, so we thought we'd try the waves on the Slimy. This was a limestone and coral reef between Cottesloe and North Cottesloe carpeted with spongy, mossy weed. Even at low tide, when only a few inches of water covered the reef, you could usually bodysurf on the Slimy, skim over it with no worse an injury than a grazed knee or stubbed toe.

I was there just for a quick surf. With my new family responsibilities, I had only an hour to spare. Of course I didn't mention this to Richie or the others. Teenage pregnancy was big news in that time and place. Even twelve months after our sudden wedding the whispering and gossiping hadn't let up, from my mother's friends, from girls I knew, even from girls I didn't know. My mother's death had only increased it. The reaction from boys wasn't so bad: just simple teasing and total incomprehension. None of them, especially a kid like Richie, would understand.

Conditions at the Slimy weren't good, but at least there was some surf: a small reef-break at the Cottesloe edge. By about three-thirty, however, the tide was rising. The surf rolling over the reef was cloudy and swirling with kelp and sand. I'd never seen so much seaweed. Then the surf began to dump heavily on the back of the reef.

There were five of us crowded out on the reef, stumbling and splashing and getting in each other's way. Richie and I started using the back of the reef as a foothold to launch ourselves into the waves breaking on the edge. The idea was that they'd carry us diagonally off the rocks and over the safer sandy-bottomed basin beyond.

This plan wasn't a success. The waves had too much water in them; the tide was too high and the waves had no shape. The water was now shoulder-deep and murky. You had to feel for the reef with your feet, thrust them blindly down into the squirming kelp and search for a crevice with your toes and heels. You had to trust your luck. Who knew what was down there? In the currents the kelp seemed alive. One moment it was pressing against you all sleek and silky, stroking your thighs and stomach, softly entwining your legs; the next it was scratching and lashing you.

We soon got tired of being buffeted by the surf and the under-tow and the rolling kelp. We were all cursing in exasperation and dancing and stumbling on the slippery weed and rocks. It was hard to get a grip on the reef, much less position yourself on a wave. And yet you needed a wave to get back to shore. To think about anything other than the next breaker and your own sudden intention was impossible. You had to concentrate.

As if conditions weren't difficult enough for bodysurfing, three board riders paddled out on heavy plywood boards and began cut-ting in on us. Those knife-nosed monsters were the last straw. They could slice right through you. With every wave-surge, one or other of us gave up and swam, rolled, and staggered through the froth to the shore. When I reached the beach I saw a straggling line of figures trudging back ahead of me along the shoreline to North Cottesloe. I headed back too. I didn't stop. I kept walking home.

NIGHT ALWAYS CHANGES THE SEA. Next morning it was calm and slick as I cruised the coast road in the Anglia, desperate for a shark story to make this humdrum Sunday day shift worthwhile. Sharks had been in the radio news that morning. There had been several "sightings" already this season.

Passing Cottesloe, I noticed four surfboats strung out in a line beyond the reef, riding the light swell. The sweep oarsman was keeping them parallel to the beach. On the boats there was no sign of physical effort or excitement. Their movements were so calm and measured they could have been fishing. As I passed, I wondered idly if the crews were trying some new training manoeuvre. One thing was sure: if they weren't rowing, they weren't chasing any sharks out to sea.

I drove farther along the West Coast Highway, and from a sandy rise where suburbanites were beginning to build new brick houses in the dunes, I looked out into the low swell. And I actually saw dark shapes gliding there. Perhaps five or six of them. Gliding, not rolling and surfacing. There was no doubt. Not dolphins, sharks. I couldn't have been more pleased.

All morning I followed them north. Then a motor sounded above the shallows. The shark-spotter plane, a little showoff Cessna, was after them too. There went my story. I could have cried. Even if the plane didn't herd them out to sea, the local surfboats would give chase. The shark alarm was already sounding back on Scarborough Beach.

I lost them then anyway, somewhere in the dunes between Scarborough and Trigg. The new breeze was just beginning to shir the surface of the ocean. Once that happened you couldn't see anything from the shore. Through the binoculars I saw the pattern and colour of the sea changing fast: small choppy waves darkening from turquoise to blue and losing their clarity. I saw that Rottnest Island had shed its mirages and returned to its proper anchorage. The sou'westerly had lifted the heat haze and brought reality back.

On the two-way, the news editor was philosophical. "You've still got a story. *Shark Pack Threatens Beaches.* Get some quotes. Over and out."

SOMEHOW MY SHARK STORY GREW from a snappy news item into an information-choked feature article. Of course I had my background material ready. My story was bursting with historical knowledge. For "colour" I dropped in a couple of quotes from the obliging Ted "Sharky" Nelson. But my coup was to bring in science.

I got "the State's leading ichthyologist," Dr. Byron McIntee, to leave his Sunday barbecue and come to the phone to declare that the sharks I'd followed up the coast were probably from the family Carcharhinidae, otherwise known as requiem sharks. Requiem sharks included some of the biggest and most voracious sharks: the tiger, whaler, bull shark, blue shark, and grey reef shark. Dr. McIntee said—and I duly wrote—they were characterized by "a nictating membrane and a heterocercal tail."

Requiem sharks were everywhere, he said. They travelled long distances each day and migrated according to seasonal changes. They had a huge range of habitat: river estuaries, tidal pools, the open ocean, muddy bays, and coral reefs. They weren't put off by fresh water or hypersalinity and were found in all tropical and temperate seas.

The biggest requiem sharks were the tigers, reaching about twenty-four feet. They were among the most important marine predators and scavengers, eating a "broad spectrum of prey": bony fishes, other sharks and rays, crustaceans, carrion, sea turtles, sea snakes, sea birds, and large marine mammals.

At last. "And humans, of course," I said.

"Let's not sensationalize that aspect."

Naturally I asked him about the name. He said that with its funereal associations *requiem* was more stirring than *tiger* or *whaler.* Exactly. I asked him to elaborate. He said it was from the obsolete French *requiem,* a variant of *requin*—"shark." And obviously influenced by the gloomier associations of the word *requiem.*

Gloomy? This was more like it.

"A requiem, as you know, is music for dead people," he said.

"So," I asked eagerly, "their name comes from their habit of killing people?" I quickly added the obligatory question: "What are the chances of a West Australian swimmer being killed by a shark?"

His sigh was loud in my ear. "You've got more chance of dying from a bee sting or a lightning strike or murder. You've got several hundred thousand times more chance of dying in a car crash on the way to the beach."

Did scientists have no imagination at all? While he talked I was thinking up a heading. *Requiem for West Australian Swimmers?* sounded pretty good to me.

He sighed again. "I hope you people aren't going to beat this thing up."

WHEN I ARRIVED BACK AT Fremantle, Dare grunted, "There you are. I need the Anglia," and sped off down Queen Street. In the two hours when his and my shifts would normally cross he was nowhere to be seen.

Next morning I was at the news agent's early to get the paper. The sub-editors had cut my thousand words to ten paragraphs. *Cut* hardly describes it. My shark story was more than filleted, more than slashed. It was *flensed*.

The story ran on page seven with a single-column, much-used stock picture of Ted "Sharky" Nelson, not a word from my ichthyologist, and the heading *Shark Hunter Warns of Beach Threat*. Dare, meanwhile, had got himself a much more important story. *Student Drowns at Cottesloe*.

How did I know his story would be about Richie Male? I felt a complete lack of surprise. It was strange how my mind abruptly turned the shock around, took it back a stage, and changed it into something like retrospective premonition.

At once my brain insisted that I'd always suspected what had happened. That I'd suspected it in the lessening of our numbers when we were out on the reef, when I kicked the weed from around my legs and stumbled ashore. And that I'd known it for sure when I saw the searching surfboats.

No, I felt no surprise at all. It seemed as if I'd known many things like this for the past year, things I'd mysteriously witnessed or hadn't acted on. Events that had slipped past me. Other people's scoops. Nor did I feel numb. Frankly, I had to struggle to keep my attention on the story. My mind was already veering toward some other narrative.

It was obvious Dare's source had been the police. The story read like a police-blotter "occurrence." It said his body, trapped in thick seaweed, had been found on Sunday afternoon by a surfboat crew in knee-deep water only fifteen yards from shore. He'd been missing since Saturday afternoon. The police thought he might have become dazed after being dumped by a wave. The police officer in charge of the search said the seaweed was so thick near the shore it was "suicidal" to swim there. The body had received a knock on the head and other abrasions, which may have been caused by rocks. It had not been disturbed by fish.

IT SOUNDS CALLOUS TO SAY that after three decades Richie's drowning, if not completely obliterated from my consciousness, had retreated into its farthest reaches. An analyst would say my imagination was still endeavouring to deal with the tragedy, however, because over twenty-five years as a novelist I had used the image of a drowned person several times in my books. I had even called a recent novel *The Drowner*, although the term *drowner* here referred chiefly to the ancient Wiltshire profession—part pragmatic rural occupation, part mystical calling—of water management. (Drowners were early irrigators, in tune with the seasons and the earth, who could divert the course of rivers at will.) Whatever my subconscious was saying—and I wouldn't deny its force for a second—for thirty years I hadn't given that Saturday afternoon a moment's conscious thought. And then suddenly I did.

While I was writing about my family and various dramatic events that occurred in Perth in the early 1960s, the memory of that day sprung from the depths, as fresh as yesterday: the cloudy light, the swirling kelp, the dirty yellow froth of the snapping waves. Now I couldn't get it out of my mind. So I wrote about that November Saturday afternoon at Cottesloe as well.

Memory is more exhausting than fiction. And so is concidence. After the memoir (which I called *The Shark Net*) was published, a businessman was killed by a white pointer shark while swimming at North Cottesloe, exactly as my teenage-reporter self had predicted (and both feared and stupidly hankered after) in the book. The attack had a curious effect on me: I took it personally; I felt shocked and deeply saddened. I couldn't dismiss it from my mind. The media was keen for me to talk and write at length about this weird coincidence.

I badly needed a break from my material and the past, and, indeed, from coincidence. I flew to Broome, in the far northwest of Western Australia, three and a half thousand kilometres from my home in Sydney, and two thousand kilometres from Perth, where the book was set and where I grew up. The nearest sizeable town to Broome is Denpasar in Bali, Indonesia. I had always wanted to go there but had never made it. It was as far as I could travel and still be in Australia.

It's not just its distance from Australia's population centres that makes Broome stand out. Overlooking Roebuck Bay, where William Dampier, the English pirate turned navigator, explorer, and chronicler of the Great South Land, careened and repaired the leaky *Roebuck* in 1699, Broome used to be a wild pearling town, with much blood spilled on its pearly white beach sand and red pindan earth. Over the years it had seen prosperity and depression, ferocious cyclones and rioting pearl divers, maritime disasters and wartime bombing. These days it is still faintly exotic, peopled by the mixed-race descendants of the old pearling industry's masters, divers, seamen, and traders: Europeans, Aborigines, Chinese, Japanese, Malays, Filipinos, Timorese, Ceylonese, Melanesians, and Arabs.

All the intensity of its history comes together at Mangrove Point, a small mangrove-fringed headland that juts out like a snub nose into the opalescent waters of Roebuck Bay at the south end of town. What initially distinguishes Mangrove Point from hundreds of similar headlands around the country's tropical northern coastline are the signs warning of a recent crocodile sighting in the area and the seasonal influx of box jellyfish ("Remove tentacles and seek urgent medical advice") and the loose scattering of unfenced graves, headstones, and unpretentious memorials known as Pioneer Cemetery.

But the dead themselves also distinguish it. Those remembered under the point's whispering sheoak trees are not the usual small-town merchants and civic bigwigs. Although several long-lived pearling masters and their families are buried in the cemetery, many here did not die of natural causes, nor were their bodies found. They were killed by the ferocity of the sea, by cyclones and sharks and divers' paralysis, and by war.

I arrived in Broome at the sweltering start of the monsoon season when the first cyclone warnings were being voiced on radio and in the *Broome Advertiser*. The same day I found myself at Mangrove Point, whose natural beauty is vivid enough to withstand the usual municipal banalities of asphalted public parking areas and cinder-block toilets, which threaten to overwhelm it. Viewed from the shade of the nearby beach café, the point's gleaming horizontal slashes of red pindan earth, green mangroves, white sand, turquoise sea, and cobalt-blue sky, so neatly framed by the rectangle of the café's veranda and roof columns, suggested the flag of some passionate tropical nation.

So indeed did the cemetery's turbulent epitaphs and histories, so far removed from the usual placid memorials of a country churchyard. Here lay Police Inspector Herbert Thomas, "whose joint effort with Captain Bardwell quelled the racial riots of 1920," a three-day battle between two thousand Japanese pearl divers and four hundred Timorese, but who collapsed and died after saving the town. Here were remembered many seamen "lost at sea" or "missing in Roebuck Bay," as well as the sixty Dutchmen and forty-five women and children, civilian refugees from the Dutch East Indies, who were machine-gunned in their seats in 1942 by strafing Japanese Zeroes while waiting for their flying boats to take off from the bay for the safety of Perth.

So fascinated was I by these highly charged memorials that at first I missed a simpler gravestone. Then I saw it. *In Loving Memory of Richard Cornelius Male. Son of Arthur Streeter and Phyllis. Brother of*

Kimberley. Passed Away 17 November, 1962. Aged 17 Years. Whom We Loved.

For several minutes I stood stunned. Richie's funeral service had been in Perth; I had assumed he'd been buried there. But of course not. He had died in the sea, and his father, the pearling master A. S. "Sam" Male, had brought him home and buried him by the sea. A pearler's life was always at risk from a multitude of disasters on and in the sea, though few would have foreseen the tragic irony of the pearling industry's youngest son drowning on a suburban beach down south in the city.

I wondered yet again if I'd had the slightest inkling he was in trouble that day, and if I could have prevented it. The mind can play tricks after all that time. With the seasons changing, a stiff breeze was rippling across the bay and the half-submerged mangroves below the point. The cemetery sheoaks whispered like graveyard trees in a movie, except the tropical sun was shining defiantly through them. I thought what a fabulous position it was up there on the headland, and what a heroic view, looking out on the timeless bay.

JENNIFER POTTER

Sacred Grove

A *fiction writer who is strongly influenced by landscape,*
JENNIFER POTTER *studied languages at Bristol University
and garden and landscape conservation at London's Architectural
Association. She has published three novels:* The Taking of
Agnès, The Long Lost Journey, *and* After Breathless.
More recently, she has turned to nonfiction as the author of
Secret Gardens *and* Lost Gardens *and as a contributor to*
The Essential Garden Book. *She has also written on gardens,
garden history, and travel for numerous periodicals.
Originator of the idea for the* Lost Gardens *television
series for Channel 4, she worked on the programs as
Associate Producer and Series Consultant.*

A MUDDY PATH VEERING OFF into rhododendron scrub, the rustle of parting leaves, a dog's distant barking, that sudden drop into silence—the memory of slipping through the cracks into Finlay's grove still raises a shiver at the back of my neck, just above the hairline.

If this were cinema, the moment would play in grainy black and white, its tension underscored by a jarringly modern soundtrack that hurts your teeth. But this experience is lived, not watched, and the silence catches me unawares. Although I hear plenty of sounds connected to my own body—thumping heart, low-pitched humming deep inside my head, day pack flapping at my back, fractionally out of time—it feels as if a muffler has dropped on me from the sky, deadening all outside sound.

Held inside the moment, you can easily lose track of where you are: in the Kröller-Müller sculpture park at Otterlo in the eastern Netherlands, where art meets nature in the woods and sandy heaths of de Hoge Veluwe, the country's largest nature reserve. I am visiting the site on a coach trip with fellow students and alumni of landscape and garden conservation at London's Architectural Association, still radical after all the years. Other trips will follow, to the gardens of Rome, Granada, Madrid, Bavaria, Berlin, Hungary, the Czech

Republic. And although I am forever haunted by visions of un-expected beauty on each of these trips—storks nesting near the ruins of La Fresneda, central Spain; overgrown cascades at the Villa Aldobrandini, Frascati—nothing has ever matched my Dutch adventure into a much duller landscape. I look to repeat it everywhere, which is probably why it never happens, and nurse a silent grudge against fellow student Gunter that its unfolding was so brutally curtailed.

The day begins much like any other: hurried breakfast, scrabble for the coach, quick check that I have all the tools for catching places on the run: camera, notebook, pencils, raincoat, umbrella, spare rolls of film, background notes (carefully annotated and underlined), itinerary. The sculpture park is our first stop. After a quick introduction to the architecture of the hunting lodge (Hollywood Gothic meets Scottish Baronial circa 1916) and a gallop around the art collection (works by Seurat, Mondrian, Corot, Van der Leck, Cézanne, van Goghs by the dozen), I slip alone into the park, where my first homage is easily paid: to Rietveld's slinky glass pavilion hovering on the lawn, a case of art sliding effortlessly into nature.

My second quarry proves stubbornly elusive, however: an installation by Scottish artist-gardener Ian Hamilton Finlay listed in the guidebook as *Five Columns for the Kröller-Müller*. Either the map is inaccurate or my map-reading skills are worse than I thought. Three times I approach the dense wall of rhododendrons marking the spot where I *think* the installation ought to be. Three times I retire, defeated, aware that time (and tour guides) wait for no one. Footsteps on the muddy path record that others have tried and failed to gain entry before me.

So I turn away too, ticking off the other sculptures and installations on my list: Claes Oldenburg's massive blue trowel tipped into the lawn, Lucio Fontana's cosmic metal balls gaping like giant clamshells among the trees, Jean Dubuffet's dazzlingly white *Jardin d'Email*, contoured in meandering stripes of thick black paint. (Here I temporarily catch up with others in my class, whom I photograph like frozen film extras, *Last Year at Marienbad* turned loopy.) Later I steal more time by jumping on an abandoned white bicycle and pedalling furiously into the woods, playing truant to myself.

Finlay unfound leaves me feeling cheated, however. As the time to leave approaches, I make a final detour by the rhododendron bank, following instinct this time instead of path or map. What happens next is both timeless and disembodied, as if it is happening to someone else. Imagine how it feels: rhododendron branches draw back the instant they are touched, and you find yourself walking through a twisted tunnel *inside* the bushes. The stems are a rich reddish-brown. Light filters dimly through toughened leaves and the smell—damp and earthy—reminds you of the dens you made at boarding school all those years ago. Half of you feels you have been here before. The other half knows you are a stranger.

But the real transformation happens when you step out of the bushes and into Finlay's grove—*Five Columns for the Kröller-Müller*, remember, except you don't see the columns straight away. What you see is what you feel, the sensation of stepping into charged space encircled by dense bushes and a tight collar of trees, forest oaks and Scots pines, the trees of your childhood in the North of England, only this is the eastern Netherlands, out of time and out of geography.

Grainy black and white bleeds slowly into dull green. Lowering skies press on your head. This is not the bright light of revelation, more the well-rubbed gleam of lived experience. You are quite alone. Even the birds have flittered away.

As you move slowly forward into the circle, you become aware of columns spaced around the edges of the clearing—suggested, really, because the artist has simply and economically attached stone plinths and bases to the bottom of five mature trees, turning each trunk into a shaft crowned with an entablature of leaves. All this you intellectualize later, along with the dominant order—Doric, you think, or Tuscan, in a mismatched medley of component parts—and the proper names carved in stone: Rousseau beneath a Scots pine; Lycurgus, Corot, Robespierre, and Michelet beneath oak. What matters at the point of entry is that sense of awe tinged with fear (as awe must always be) when you connect with a reality that is greater than you.

And I was frightened, believe me. It felt like the scene of a crime—a place of ritual sacrifice, at least.

MEMORY HAS A WAY OF appropriating an image like a bad Polaroid, forever fixed at the moment the shutter closed. I am standing stock-still in the clearing, head cocked, heart beating, face clenched into a frown . . . In the movie of shocks and suspense, this is the long strung-out moment before the nasty surprise pops up from the scrub, making every member of the audience jump out of his or her red plush seat. But I must unfreeze the frame, nudge the memory a little to left and right, if I am ever to understand why Finlay's grove has tracked me down the years to the point at which I can close my eyes and step into the space where hearts beat faster and hairs really do stand on end.

I know immediately where to start looking: in another grove, in south London's Maryon Park, close to the Thames at Woolwich.

Although I saw it first in a film, I have visited this landscape every few years to see if it still snags me in the same way (it always does). The film is Antonioni's *Blowup*, shot at the start of my student years and very much of its time: swinging London; red double-decker buses; skimpy skirts worn over baby-pink tights; the fashion photographer as icon of modernity, fluid, hip, snap-happy indoors and out; handbags everywhere.

In an otherwise deserted corner of the park, the photographer-hero snaps a courting couple embracing on a grassy knoll surrounded by bushes and trees. Only later, as he develops the film, does he begin to suspect that what he witnessed was murder, not love. He photographs his own photographs to make sure. A body appears, then disappears from the undergrowth. White-faced mime artists play tennis with nonexistent balls in a cinematic pun on different kinds of reality. The film itself goes missing. No photographs, no crime.

Yes, Maryon Park viewed through the iris of Michelangelo Antonioni's lens looked and felt exactly like Finlay's grove.

There were minor differences, of course. The grassy knoll in south London is enclosed by a palisade fence. The London trees are not so tall and have not been turned into art. An obtrusive housing block scarcely seen in the movie dominates one corner, though you could always pretend it wasn't there. Apart from that, I got the same shiver from each. Heard the same soundtrack (birds, trees, wind, leaves, distant dogs). Experienced the same lurch into silence. Looked at least in retrospect for the hand in the bushes pointing the gun toward the couple embracing under the trees, the older man manoeuvred straight into the line of fire.

The more I think about it, the more this worries me. Maryon Park I obviously saw through Antonioni's eyes, but did I then look at a Dutch landscape through the eyes of an Italian film director looking at an unremarkable London park? Are the images I have retained of Finlay's grove tainted, like false memories, recovered from someone else's brain? Landscape, memory, art—the overlays have got me confused, unable to recall either what I saw or what I really remember. I write novels inspired by landscape and garden books inspired by art, but I wonder if I shouldn't keep them apart—give places back the power simply to be, without trying to turn them into something else. Having long admired Finlay's subversive blend of artistic gardening, I now wonder if his shock tactics and sly cultural asides are not part of the problem. *Certain gardens are described as retreats when they are really attacks*—you see what I mean?

And maybe photography itself is to blame for my difficulty in teasing out what happened that day. We rarely bother to look any-more; the camera does that for us. But it does not—cannot—experience the wild as we do. Camera images cannot stretch over your head and around your back. They don't stick in your ears or lodge in your throat. You don't sit in them like you do in the world, and how-ever many shots you take, there will always be bits missing (usually the best bits because that's how we are). I find it significant that I took no photographs in Finlay's grove. This gives me a clue that something really did happen that day to disturb my fixed habits of aim, shoot, and leave the looking until last. But without the camera's substantiating evidence, how can I possibly discover its cause? Was it nature or art that set my pulse racing, the wild or the tamed, or something in between?

LOOKING AT LANDSCAPE THROUGH the artist's manipulating vision is a trick we have learned over the centuries, as painted land-scapes developed into a respectable genre beyond the record of mere possession. In Georgian England, the landscape garden's sculptured hillocks, serpentine lakes, and Arcadian temples owed much of their inspiration to Claude Lorrain's gilded scenes painted a century or so earlier. As landscape tastes grew wilder, the first tourists equipped themselves with the perfect device for reducing the rough edges of nature to a Claudian composition. Faced with a sylvan view or rough mountain scene, you needed only your "Claude glass"—a little convex mirror, convenient as a powder compact—to compose your "picture." It worked best if you looked backwards over your shoulder, removing yourself as far as possible from the actual scene.

The effect was undoubtedly similar to viewing a landscape projected through a camera obscura, like the one I visited in Bristol, built by an artist (who else?) up on Clifton Down. You saw the rustling trees from across the gorge reflected on a white dish—saw them in tremendous detail, like leaves in a movie—and you waited for the soundtrack to begin (birds, trees, wind, leaves, distant dogs). When no sound came you felt vaguely cheated, even though intellectually you knew that these were real leaves, not movie leaves at all.

The trouble with looking at landscape through someone else's directed vision is that it quickly removes the need to see and respond for yourself. I spent much of my childhood in the Lake District, eventually moving to a stone cottage in the shadow of Rydal Mount, where William Wordsworth lived out the last long years of his life. On the adjoining Rydal Hall estates were two ordinary waterfalls that were singled out for extravagant praise by all the late-eighteenth-century tourists from Thomas Gray and the Reverend William Gilpin onward. Both doubtless pranced about the stones looking back at the "awful and sublime" falls through their Claude glasses, which magnified the falls' drama as they codified the scene.

I didn't know this as a child. The falls were simply part of my every-day landscape, and better for it, too. I saw them with my own eyes, not anyone else's.

But seeing with my own eyes grew harder as I grew older, travelled farther afield, read more widely, saw many more movies whose emotions I projected onto otherwise unsullied landscapes. When my father's work took him to Jordan on a water aid project funded by the World Bank, I visited there one winter and drove with my parents through Lawrence of Arabia country to the desert police outpost at Wadi Rum. The slow drive down from Amman, with looping detours to Ma'dabā and Karak, gave me my first real taste of the desert. Until then, the landscapes I knew intimately were modelled to a human scale: the smallness of English counties and of Cumbria's glaciated valleys, lakes scooped into their crevices, fells tight as fists. Here in Jordan, baked earth stretched endlessly in all directions, abutting distant land formations beyond chimerical lakes created by the heat haze. Yet instead of feeling crushed by such obvious proof of my own insignificance, I felt giddy, freed from the absurd chore of having to make my mark on the world. In the desert vastness, my day-to-day concerns simply didn't matter anymore.

And of course I was stepping into familiar territory, both filmic and literary: David Lean's great desert movie, *Lawrence of Arabia*, Peter O'Toole in Arab headdress, lips quivering at the Turkish brutality of Deraa; Lawrence himself in *Seven Pillars of Wisdom*, his classic account of the Arab revolt against the Turks. With Lawrence I could drink open-mouthed of the "effortless, empty, eddyless wind of the desert, throbbing past," and with David Lean's magnificent cinemascope images in my head, I could swap the jeep and my parents for Lawrence's caravan of camels advancing down the flat-bottomed valley of Wadi Rum toward the police post that was our goal. "Our little caravan grew self-conscious," writes Lawrence of this very same landscape, "and fell dead quiet, afraid and ashamed to flaunt its smallness in the presence of the stupendous hills." Did I feel small only after I read that description, or did my reading of Lawrence confirm the way I had felt for myself? After so many years it's hard to unravel which came first and whether I properly saw or felt anything at all.

But at least I have a stack of faded transparencies to remind me of our progress down the magnificent valley of Wadi Rum—the sections of red-rock walls on either side like city blocks, stained and cut with alleys and capped with shallow domes, Byzantine in effect, ceremonial in scale. The police post is suitably picturesque, small and chunky, looking out across a cultivated strip of tufty grass, weathered edging stones, and scrubby young trees—eucalyptus and what looks like dusty cypress, no more than a memory of how a garden might be. I have photographs too, of people: Father looking smug on a camel; handsome, eager children from the Bedouin encampment; Mother looking smug on a camel; two of me executing a kind of dance in the desert (to Maurice Jarre's stirring soundtrack?) wearing a checked miniskirt, cream sweater, and creamy kid leather boots. I clearly hadn't yet acquired a sense of appropriate dress. The way I am holding up my arms reminds me of the model girls in *Blowup*, though I can only assume the echo was unintended unless everything really is connected to everything else.

From that day I carried a very British nostalgia for desert spaces that eventually turned into a novel when I stepped off an underground train at London's Victoria Station and walked straight into a poster advertising the desert landscapes of Victorian painter David

Roberts then on show. I still had to find the precise desert land (the Yemen) and the characters (Gertrude Bell meets a cross between gun-running French poet Arthur Rimbaud and actor Sean Connery) before the story could begin to flow. But landscape provided the initial inspiration.

What happened in Jordan is one variant of the way culture seeps into nature, making it hard (unless we are very clear-headed) to see anything afresh. Finlay's intention in his grove was more intentionally subversive, however. The Roman collars he snapped onto the five forest trees around the edges of the rhododendron grove bring Culture and Nature into direct confrontation. Sparks fly from the friction between them, producing the shivers that shot up and down my spine as soon as I pushed my way into the empty space.

Lacking any shots of my own of Finlay's grove, I must trust to memory and what I can read into the artist's intentions if I am to understand what happened to me that day in the Otterlo hunting forest. Finlay, I know, is a political maverick who likes nothing better than a good scrap. He would surely subscribe to Susan Sontag's maxim in her celebrated essay "Against Interpretation" that "real art has the capacity to make us nervous," because that's what he clearly set out to do in the Otterlo forest: make us nervous as we slide into his empty trap.

His strategy works on me, at least, when I finally push my way through into the grove. The columns make me uneasy because they conjoin separate parts of my life, childhood trees and adult stones, nature and architecture, the near and the distant past brought together in a present curiously out of time. Scraps of art-and-garden history fizz about in my head. French priest and neoclassicist Abbé Laugier turned trees into stone with his notion that the primitive hut inspired the architectural column, and here comes Finlay turning stones into trees. What he means by the names carved onto his columns is less clear, however. Together they form an odd bunch of hot- and cold-blooded radicals whose professions span philosophy, law, politics, history, and art. Two in particular connect to my sense of self and history: Robespierre and Rousseau, both French (if you discount Rousseau's Swiss birth), a connection to my days as a student of French at Bristol and the Sorbonne.

Radical Jacobin Maximilien François Marie Isidore de Robespierre helped to secure the execution of Louis xvi at the start of the French Revolution, thereby unleashing the Terror that claimed a mountain of guillotined heads before Robespierre's own was chopped off in July 1794. My personal connection to Robespierre has nothing to do with a chopped-off head, however. For reasons I never understood, Le Monde once labelled my film-director husband the Robespierre of English cinema. Our marriage had ended just a few months before the Netherlands trip, and here he was, leaping out at me from the plinth to a mock Roman column on the edge of a rhododendron thicket. I could only hope it was not an omen.

Like Robespierre and the Terror, Jean-Jacques Rousseau crops up continually in Finlay's work and in my own fascination for the artful wild. He appears eminently modern in his ability to hold two conflicting ideas in his head and argue both with equal force. A passionate advocate of the emotional education of children, Rousseau passed his own illegitimate offspring straight on to a foundling hospital, as if the Rights of Man applied to everyone except his own flesh and blood. Finlay's verdict, written on a prettily illustrated card, strikes me as apt. "Both the garden style called 'sentimental', and the French Revolution, grew from Rousseau. The garden trellis, and the guillotine, are alike entwined with the honeysuckle of the new 'sensibility'." In the accompanying image, flowering honeysuckle transforms a rustic guillotine into a garden arch.

Rousseau's thoughts and writings influenced whole generations of Romantics, not least the garden makers of the eighteenth and nineteenth centuries, who gradually succumbed to his admiration for unspoilt nature and to his passion for collecting wildflowers and grasses. Julie's garden in *La Nouvelle Héloise* is a wilderness, its artfulness concealed in scrupulous meadow planting and foaming brooks that look as nature intended, quite unlike Finlay, who pins his art to his sleeve. Yet I wonder if the proponents of artifice and iconography didn't get the last laugh at the fate of Rousseau's Roman tomb, ringed with poplars on its island setting at the marquis de Girardin's landscaped estate of Ermenonville, France. After Rousseau's sudden death, his tomb became a stock garden feature, mimicked across Europe in Poland, Germany, the Czech Republic. One glimpse of encircling poplars reflected atmospherically in a lake was all it took to evoke the appropriate response. *Man was born free and is everywhere in chains* . . . Or maybe that other revolutionary slogan shared with Robespierre, his disciple in many things: *liberty, equality, fraternity*, a trinity of ideals that transmuted during the Terror into the ever more chilling *liberty, equality, or death*.

I see I have left the most important element till last: the empty space at the heart of the grove itself.

My dictionary defines *grove* as a small wood, an orchard, or a group of trees—classically the olive tree, small, gnarled, and silver leaved, set in orchard rows on the productive slopes of Tuscany, scattered and venerable in the Roman *campagna* at Tivoli ("Beware the vipers in the long grass," warned our Italian guide, Alessandro, who sang the virtues of "middle-aged villages" up in the hills). But if the grove describes the trees, I see them always wrapped around a clearing that is more properly the province of man.

Apart from the Kröller-Müller, most of the groves I know are benign. Groves offer sanctuary, a respite from the dark slitherings of the forest. It is where children feel safe enough to play before they are tricked and trapped by the wicked witch, and where young people come when they want to be alone. Since the time of the Greeks, worship has been one of the grove's more social functions. In the woods of northeastern Pennsylvania, I have sat with Quakers in a pine grove, listening for warblers and the clear sweet call of the hermit thrush, while lending half an ear to the testimonies of Friends. Their words came and went, but the memory of sitting in dappled sunlight under the soaring pines remains strong.

After the service, I lingered on my rough wooden bench until the last of the worshippers had gone. The benches, three deep, were set in a square around an empty space. To one side was a raised platform just large enough to hold a rustic armchair and sofa. The bentwood furniture reminded me of another art installation in another forest —Richard Caink's *Habitat* in the Grizedale Forest west of Lake Windermere. In the Cumbrian clearing Caink has placed the trappings of an ordinary English living room but carved out of solid wood—sofa, pelmeted curtains, TV set, and standard lamp. His "meaning," so my guide map explained, "is to articulate notions of our relationship to the natural world," taking the familiar out into the woods, "where our origins lie, or at least reminding us we are still embedded within the fabric of nature."

This mania for seeing links, making connections, layering one experience over another—can we no longer experience anything in the raw? Must nature always be mediated by art and quite possibly vice versa? Must I wait for the photographs to be developed before I know what I have seen and felt?

I want to give the grove one last try, to recollect (as rawly as I can) the experience of slipping from the known into the unknown, from the cultivated (and cultured) into the wild.

These are the elements that conspired to send shivers up and down the back of my neck that day in the Otterlo hunting forest: an unreliable map; a hidden path you had to find for yourself; a sudden embouchement into empty space ringed with dense rhododendron bushes and mature trees, five of which had been turned into Roman columns by stone plinths attached to their bases; five names that together spelled landscape, liberty, and losing your head, not necessarily in that order. Here is a classic scenario for initiation into a mystery. I did not know then—I swear it—that although my map referred to Finlay's installation as *Five Columns for the Kröller-Müller*, its more usual name is Sacred Grove.

I am pushing my way through the rhododendron scrub. In contrast to my previous attempts, the branches are pliant to my will, almost as if they want to bend backward of their own accord. They certainly don't swing back to slap me in the face. The moment of stepping through the bushes into the grey-green space of the clearing stretches like elastic so that I experience the transformation in the slowest of motions, darkness into light, lost into found, humdrum into supranormal. In that moment I experience both panic and its opposite—an absolute conviction that whatever happens is a product of my will.

I shall resist the writer's urge to tell you what the experience was *like*. It was like itself, that's all, stripped down and pure. I feel my body all over, and the boundaries of my skin, but I also feel transparently insubstantial. It is possible to hold two conflicting ideas in your head, just as it is possible to experience two contradictory sensations in a single moment. Hot feels cold. Red looks green. Joy makes you cry. Skin and not-skin feel just the same to me. Time has stood still, or at least fails to register. "Where does time go when it's gone?" is a question put to me once by my puzzling son. "Finlay's grove," I should have said. "That's where time goes when it's spent."

Somewhere on the periphery of my vision are five sacred trees (four oaks and a Scots pine) and five column bases, glimpsed as a blur. My eyes have turned fisheye to hold them in view. I am quivering all over, which is hardly surprising. Sacrifices do that to you, whether you intend to wield the knife or put your own head on the block. A noise is whining in my head, getting louder all the time.

What is most remarkable, though, is my heightened sensitivity to detail rather than space. I have never looked like this before—looked and *seen* the natural objects lying all around. The upper surface of each rhododendron leaf has a dull dark gleam, darker than its duller underside, which has no gleam at all. Dead leaves lie hard and brown on the springy floor, rolled into tubes. The clustering trunks are fluid, twisted and held in a spring. Beyond the bushes, the grass is painfully green—pure grass-green, like nothing else. The bark on the oak is ridged and knobbly, deeply fissured; its colours are grey, brown, occasional lighter ash. The Scots pine is pinker, scabs of bark layered in different colours: grey, pink, rust, occasional brown. If I am about to lose my head, it's not my life that flashes before my eyes but a minutiae of leaves, grass, trees, and sky. Mesmerized by single blades of grass, I feel the greyness lifting out of the sky as bands of brightness show through—so bright I cover my eyes with my hands . . .

The pain and joy of really looking hits me hard. I am walking slowly into the grove's inner core, held in the silence that grows more intense the deeper I go. Fear slips away. I almost forget to breathe.

Here is the heart of the mystery. I am standing on the edge, about to plunge inside, when I hear a sudden crashing behind my back and my friend Gunter blunders through the bushes. A student from an earlier year, Gunter's enthusiasm is legendary, as is his determination to devour ideas, culture, artifacts, anything that matters.

He sees me standing all alone before the five Roman columns, body tensed.

Out comes his camera, top of the range, and a fancy lens, which he snaps into place.

"Wunderful," says Gunter. "Truly wunderful. Excuse me please . . ."

I step aside to give him a better view. "Look at those *columns* . . . Shit . . . The lens, it won't stretch far enough wide . . . Oh yes . . . that's it."

He shoots off a dozen or more frames, striding round the grove on rubbery legs to hit the right angle. I am by now thrust to the clearing's edge. A bird sings loudly then a plane passes overhead. The barking dog moves closer. It's no use. Gunter has chased away whatever I was about to discover. The light loses its clarity and so do I.

Without a word to Gunter, I turn and push my way back through the bushes. The path seems obvious, now that I know where to look. In fifteen minutes I am back on the coach, a little breathless, seated dead-centre right at the back looking up the aisle.

Gunter keeps us waiting, but at least I have time to check my equipment for the next site, the restored royal palace at Het Loo. Camera, notebook, pencils, spare rolls of film, raincoat, umbrella. I'll need those last two. The clouds have rolled back in and a light rain has started to fall. I shall be hungry by teatime. Before I sleep, though, I shall study tomorrow's itinerary, making plenty of notes. It is important to know where you are headed, always. The rain intensifies as we sit and wait for Gunter's return. I load another film into my camera, just in case.

DAVID QUAMMEN

The Same River Twice

STENOTHERMAL WATERS AND THE
REMORSELESS FLOW OF TIME

DAVID QUAMMEN *is a two-time* National Magazine Award *winner for his science essays and other work in* Outside *magazine. The author of three novels and several other books, including* Wild Thoughts from Wild Places *and* The Song of the Dodo, *he is the recipient of an Academy Award in literature from the American Academy of Arts and Letters. He lives in Montana.*

ONE OF THE CHIEF MERITS *of the short personal essay as a literary form,* *I've long believed, is that it allows a writer to juxtapose and connect disparate* *elements—facts, ideas, creatures, memories, times, places, fields of knowl-* *edge—that seem utterly unrelated. The essayist, unlike other journalists, is* *granted a certain blessed latitude to perform as a verbal collage artist, taking* *fragments of material from the world, a bit of this, a bit of that, and pasting* *them together into fresh, unexpected patterns of meaning. The result in each* *case is a sort of extended oxymoron. The only valid standard of judgement is* not Do these things logically belong together? *but* Does the mix somehow work?

The following essay lurked in my mind, as a blurry, incomplete notion *and a kind of unhealed sorrow, for a number of years before I wrote it. Most* *of the elements were there. I had the recollection of an extraordinary situa-* *tion of friendship, and a sad, helpless sense of regret at its loss. I had a pass-* *ing familiarity with Heraclitus and his most famous dictum, though I had* *never given serious attention to his work. I had some training in aquatic ento-* *mology—enough to know one species of stonefly from another. And I was* *aware that the steady, unvarying environment of a spring creek differs conse-* *quentially from the hectic, variable life of a meltwater river. But one* *element of my potential collage was missing. I had never seen spring creek* *ecology described in the rigorous, quantifying terms of science.*

Then, one day, I stumbled across an obscure paper in a 1964 volume of the journal Ecology. *The author was a scientist named Clark Hubbs, about whom I knew nothing. The title was "Effects of Thermal Fluctuations on the Relative Survival of Greenthroat Darter Young from Stenothermal and Eurythermal Waters." The very word* stenothermal *gave me a firm grip on a central concept, and from Hubbs I went back to Heraclitus. Suddenly it was possible to say what I thought and felt.*

I'VE BEEN READING HERACLITUS this week, so naturally my brain is full of river water.

Heraclitus, you'll recall, was the Greek philosopher of the sixth century B.C. who gets credit for having said: "You cannot step twice into the same river." Heraclitus was a loner, according to the sketchy accounts of him, and rather a crank. He lived in the town of Ephesus, near the coast of Asia Minor opposite mainland Greece, not far from a great river that in those days was called the Meander. He never founded a philosophic school, like Plato and Pythagoras did. He didn't want followers. He simply wrote his one book and deposited the scroll in a certain sacred building, the temple of Artemis, where the general public couldn't get hold of it. The book itself was eventually lost, and all that survives of it today are about a hundred fragments, which have come down secondhand in the works of other ancient writers. So his ideas are known only by hearsay. He seems to have said a lot of interesting things, some of them cryptic, some of them downright ornery, but his river comment is the one for which Heraclitus is widely remembered. The full translation is: "You cannot step twice into the same river, for other waters are continually flowing on." To most people it comes across as a nice resonant metaphor, a bit of philosophic poetry. To me it is that and more.

Once, for a stretch of years, I lived in a very small town on the bank of a famous Montana river. It was famous mainly for its trout, this river, and for its clear water and its abundance of chemical nutrients, and for the seasonal blizzards of emerging insects that made it one of the most rewarding pieces of habitat in North America, arguably in the world, if you happened to be a trout or a fly-fisherman. I happened to be a fly-fisherman.

One species of insect in particular—one "hatch," to use the slightly misleading term that fishermen apply to these impressive entomological events, when a few billion members of some mayfly or stonefly or caddisfly species all emerge simultaneously into adulthood and take flight over a river—one insect hatch in particular gave this river an unmatched renown. The species was *Pteronarcys californica*, a monstrous but benign stonefly that grew more than two inches long and carried a pinkish-orange underbelly for which it had gotten the common name "salmonfly." These insects, during their three years of development as aquatic larvae, could survive only in a river that was cold, pure, fast-flowing, rich in dissolved oxygen, and covered across its bed with boulders the size of bowling balls, among which the larvae would live and graze. The famous river offered all those conditions extravagantly, and so *P. californica* flourished there, like nowhere else. Trout flourished in turn.

When the clouds of *P. californica* took flight, and mated in air, and then began dropping back onto the water, the fish fed upon them voraciously, recklessly. Wary old brown trout the size of a person's thigh, granddaddy animals that would never otherwise condescend to feed by daylight upon floating insects, came up off the bottom for this banquet. Each gulp of *P. californica* was a major nutritional windfall. The trout filled their bellies and their mouths and still continued gorging. Consequently the so-called salmonfly so-called hatch on this river, occurring annually during two weeks in June, triggered by small changes in water temperature, became a wild and garish national festival in the fly-fishing year. Stockbrokers in New York, corporate lawyers in San Francisco, federal judges and star-quality surgeons and foundation presidents—the sort of folk who own antique bamboo fly rods and field jackets of Irish tweed—planned their vacations around this event. They packed their gear and then waited for the telephone signal from a guide in a shop on Main Street of the little town where I lived.

The signal would say: *It's started.* Or, in more detail: *Yeah, the hatch is on. Passed through town yesterday. Bugs everywhere. By now the head end of it must be halfway to Varney Bridge. Get here as soon as you can.* They got there. Cab drivers and schoolteachers came too. People who couldn't afford to hire a guide and be chauffeured comfortably in a Mackenzie boat, or who didn't want to, arrived with dinghies and johnboats lashed to the roofs of old yellow buses. And if the weather held, and you got yourself to the right stretch of river at the right time, it could indeed be very damn good fishing.

But that wasn't why I lived in the town. Truth be known, when *P. californica* filled the sky and a flotilla of boats filled the river, I usually headed in the opposite direction. I didn't care for the crowds. It was almost as bad as the Fourth of July rodeo, when the town suddenly became clogged with college kids from a nearby city, and Main Street was ankle deep in beer cans on the morning of the fifth, and I would find people I didn't know sleeping it off in my front yard, under the scraggly elm. The salmonfly hatch was like that, only with stockbrokers and flying hooks. Besides, there were other places and other ways to catch fish. I would take my rod and my waders and disappear to a small spring creek that ran through a stock ranch on the bottomland east of the river.

It was private property. There was no room for guided boats on this little creek, and there was no room for tweed. Instead of tweed there were sheep—usually about thirty head, bleating in halfhearted annoyance but shuffling out of my way as I hiked from the barn out to the water. There was an old swayback horse named Buck, a buckskin; also a younger one, a hot white-stockinged mare that had once been a queen of the barrel-racing circuit and hadn't forgotten her previous station in life. There was a graveyard of rusty car bodies, a string of them, DeSotos and Fords from the Truman years, dumped into the spring creek along one bend to hold the bank in place and save the sheep pasture from turning into an island. Locally this sort of thing is referred to as the "Detroit riprap" mode of soil conservation; after a while, the derelict cars come to seem a harmonious part of the scenery. There was also an old two-storey ranch house of stucco, with yellow trim. Inside lived a man and a woman, married then.

Now we have come to the reason I did live in that town. Actually there wasn't one reason but three: the spring creek, the man, and the woman. At the time, for a stretch of years, those were three of the closest friends I'd ever had.

This spring creek was not one of the most eminent Montana spring creeks, not Nelson Spring Creek and not Armstrong, not the sort of place where you could plunk down twenty-five dollars per rod per day for the privilege of casting your fly over large savvy trout along an exclusive and well-manicured section of water. On this creek you fished free or not at all. I fished free, because I knew the two people inside the house and, through them, the wonderful surly old rancher who owned the place.

They lived there themselves, those two, in large part because of the creek. The male half of the partnership was at that time a raving and insatiable fly-fisherman, like me, for whom the luxury of having this particular spring creek just a three-minute stroll from his back door was worth any number of professional and personal sacrifices. He had found a place he loved dearly, and he wanted to stay. During previous incarnations he had been a wire-service reporter in Africa, a bar owner in Chicago, a magazine editor in New York, a reform-school guard in Idaho, and a timber-faller in the winter woods of Montana. He had decided to quit the last before he cut off a leg with his chain saw, or worse; he was later kind enough to offer me his saw and his expert coaching and then to dissuade me deftly from making use of either, during the period when I was so desperate and foolhardy as to consider trying to earn a living that way. All we both wanted, really, was to write novels and fly-fish for trout. We fished the spring creek, together and individually, more than a hundred days each year. We memorized that water. The female half of the partnership, on the other hand, was a vegetarian by principle who lived chiefly on grapefruit and considered that anyone who tormented innocent fish—either for food or, worse, for the sport of catching them and then gently releasing them, as we did—showed the most inexcusable symptoms of arrested development and demented adolescent cruelty, but she tolerated us. All she wanted was to write novels and read Jane Austen and ride the hot mare. None of us had any money.

None of us was being published. Nothing happened in that town between October and May. The man and I played chess. We endangered our lives hilariously cutting and hauling firewood. We skied into the backcountry carrying tents and cast-iron skillets and bottles of wine, then argued drunkenly over whether it was proper to litter the woods with eggshells, if the magpies and crows did it too. We watched Willie Stargell win a World Series. Sometimes on cold clear days we put on wool gloves with no fingertips and went out to fish. Meanwhile the woman sequestered herself in a rickety backyard shed, with a small wood stove and a cot and a manual typewriter, surrounded by black widow spiders that she chose to view as pets. Or the three of us stood in their kitchen, until late hours on winter nights, while the woman peeled and ate uncountable grapefruits and the man and I drank whiskey, and we screamed at each other about literature.

The spring creek ran cool in summer. It ran warm in winter. This is what spring creeks do; this is their special felicity. It steamed and it rippled with fluid life when the main river was frozen over solid. Anchor ice never formed on the rocks of its riffles, killing insect larvae where they lived, and frazil ice never made the water slushy—as occurred on the main river. During spring runoff this creek didn't flood; therefore the bottom wasn't scoured and disrupted, and the eggs of the rainbow trout, which spawned around that time, weren't swept out of the nests and buried lethally in silt. The creek did go brown with turbidity during runoff, from the discharge of several small tributaries that carried meltwater out of the mountains through an erosional zone, but the colour would clear again soon.

Insects continued hatching on this creek through the coldest months of the winter. In October and November, large brown trout came upstream from the main river and scooped out their spawning nests on a bend that curved around the sheep pasture, just downstream from the car bodies. In August, grasshoppers blundered onto the water from the brushy banks, and fish exploded out of nowhere to take them. Occasionally I or the other fellow would cast a tiny fly and pull in a grayling, that gorgeous and delicate cousin of trout, an

Arctic species left behind by the last glaciation that fared poorly in the warm summer temperatures of sun-heated meltwater rivers. In this creek a grayling could be comfortable, because most of the water came from deep underground. That water ran cool in summer, relatively, and warm in winter, relatively—relative in each case to the surrounding air temperature, as well as the temperature of the main river. In absolute terms the creek's temperature tended to be stable year-round, holding steady in a hospitable middle range close to the constant temperature of the groundwater from which it was fed. This is what spring creeks, by definition, do. The scientific jargon for such a balanced condition is *stenothermal*: temperatures in a narrow range. The ecological result is a stable habitat and a twelve-month growing season. Free from extremes of cold or heat, free from flooding, free from ice and heavy siltation and scouring, the particular spring creek in question seemed always to me a thing of sublime and succouring constancy. In that regard it was no different from other spring creeks; but it was the one I knew and cared about.

The stretch of years came to an end. The marriage came to an end. There were reasons, but the reasons were private, and are certainly none of our business here. Books were pulled down off shelves and sorted into two piles. Fine oaken furniture, too heavy to be hauled into uncertain futures, was sold off for the price of a sad song. The white-stockinged mare was sold also, to a family with a couple of young barrel-racers, and the herd of trap-lame and half-feral cats was divided up. The man and the woman left town individually, in separate trucks, at separate times, each headed back toward New York City. I helped load the second truck, the man's, but my voice wasn't functioning well on that occasion. I was afflicted with a charley horse of the throat. It had all been hard to witness, not simply because a marriage had ended but even more so because, in my unsolicited judgement, a great love affair had. This partnership of theirs had been a vivid and imposing thing.

Or maybe it was hard because two love affairs had ended—if you count mine with the pair of them. I should say here that a friendship remains between me and each of them. Friendship with such folk is a lot. But it's not the same.

Now I live in the city from which college students flock off to the Fourth of July rodeo in that little town, where they raise hell for a day and litter Main Street with beer cans and then sleep it off under the scraggly elm in what is now someone else's front yard—the compensation being that July Fourth is quieter up here. It is only an hour's drive.

Not too long ago I was down there myself. I parked, as always, in the yard by the burn barrel outside the stucco house. The house was empty; I avoided it. With my waders and my fly rod I walked out to the spring creek. Of course it was all a mistake.

I stepped into the creek and began fishing my way upstream, casting a grasshopper imitation into patches of shade along the overhung banks. There were a few strikes. There was a fish caught and released. But after less than an hour I quit. I climbed out of the water. I left. I had imagined that a spring creek was a thing of sublime and succouring constancy. I was wrong. Heraclitus was right.

SHARON BUTALA

Living Inside the Landscape

SHARON BUTALA *is the author of* Wild Stone Heart,
The Perfection of the Morning, *and many other books
and articles comprising various genres. She has received
numerous awards and prizes for her writing, and three of
her books were on the Canadian bestseller lists for extended
periods of time. She has also been the recipient with her
husband of many nature conservation awards.*

MY SON (MY FIRST and only child) was about three months old and, unfortunately, one of those babies who never sleep more than an hour or two at a time. One evening when he was in his crib and if not actually asleep at least quiet, I took advantage of this rare lull to stagger into the bedroom and fall onto our bed for a quick nap.

I was only twenty-three, and an uncertain, even a frightened young woman, struggling, at the same time as I was coming to terms with being a mother and the sole support of my family, to establish the career I'd so long dreamt of. The truth is, I didn't really know what I was doing in any area of my life, as wife, mother, teacher, person, although occasionally I thought I did, which was usually when I did the most damage. That I understood virtually nothing about life, or so it seems to me now, and even less about myself, is not an aside to this story.

The next thing I remember about that long-ago evening was that I opened my eyes, and although I knew immediately that I was in our bedroom in our small frame house in a tiny prairie town, I felt that I had been away, that I had been somewhere else, and I didn't know where that was or how that could be possible. In my bewilderment, grasping for an anchor, I called out to my husband, who was studying in the dining room. After a moment, he opened the bed-room door—I remember his dark silhouette against the too-bright light in the other room—and I asked him, as if this would straighten everything out, how long I'd been asleep.

"Oh, about a half hour," he said. "Why?"

"I had a . . . dream," I said. "That is, I think it was a dream."

He sat down on the bed beside me in the semidarkness and listened as I struggled to tell him what I had just seen: The back yard of our house as it actually was in waking life—the narrow, cracked cement sidewalk set in the lawn, the shabby white picket fence crossing it at right angles, a row of old, tall trees—poplars, I think—on the other side of the fence, and the baby asleep in his carriage, which sat on the grass beside the sidewalk—a sidewalk that now was ugly and dead, a brutal scar in the scene.

I tried to describe to him the essence of this picture, how the blue sky behind and above the trees, and their leaves and their leaning, gnarled grey trunks, and the vivid green grass, and the baby, *were all made of the same material*, that all the things that we would say were living, were, without distinction, made of the same substance. There was no room for doubt about this message; it was absolutely, indisputably true. It was beyond true—it simply *was* how the universe is.

He wanted to know more details, and with difficulty I managed to step back a little from the experience and to tell him about the intense, otherworldly beauty, the scintillating colours, and the stillness—how still everything in the picture was. In time, I added that the scene was imbued with a perfect peace, with what I *thought* was an air of benevolence permeating it—but not love; love had nothing to do with it. As well, I had a sense, which still remains with me, of the trees as having—what?—a quality of listening? Of waiting? As if they had knowledge, intelligence, wisdom—I can't say what exactly. I think, at the very least, they had consciousness.

My husband was a student of Eastern philosophies, and he identified my dream—by this time I was calling it a vision—almost at once as something he'd read about, as an experience that although it has other names, is usually referred to as the vision of Universal Oneness. He said that it was not unique to me, that versions of it have been reported in many religions—Christianity, Hinduism, Judaism, Islam, Buddhism, Taoism—and that through the ages around the world books had been written about it, that skeptics had, nevertheless, denied it, yet its ubiquitousness had given even the skeptics pause.

I have some memory of lying there for a few moments longer, still immersed in that wonderful picture, amazed and full of gratitude that such an astonishing thing could happen to someone as inconsequential as I then felt myself to be. But, I'm sure, the baby began to cry, wanting changing or feeding, and I had to prepare for work the next morning, and so the rest of the evening has vanished from my memory. I think that I was so stunned by what had happened to me that for a long time I couldn't really think about it; I could only remember it and mentally replay it.

As I went about my life, though, as might be expected, the immediacy of the vision diminished until I was finally able to think about its meaning. I felt sure that to have seen such a thing should change my life. But no matter how much I mulled over what I had seen, I could make no sense of it. Despite its absolute authority, which I could not deny even years later, it was beyond my ability to comprehend that my most precious child could be made of the same material as the grass or the trees. I would have simply rejected this message, but the vision's power always, at the last moment, held me back from full denial. I thought, there must be some other meaning, some other way of interpreting this, which I just haven't seen yet, and I puzzled over the vision in this other light, as having meaning that I just hadn't yet figured out.

Time passed, life began to be variously too busy, too difficult, too grindingly sad, or too exhilarating, and in all this excitement and pleasure and sometimes despair, my vision (and my inability to assimilate it) receded further and further from my thoughts. In this way fifteen and then twenty years passed, during which I occasionally remembered it, and before forgetting it, pondered briefly again the strange, beautiful vision I had had when I was twenty-three.

I WAS BORN IN A VILLAGE just south of the boreal forest of Saskatchewan. My parents were not settlers; my father had a sawmill that had, periodically, to be moved, but we were located northwest of the village, and my mother came down out of "the bush," as it is still called, to give birth to her babies in the village's Red Cross outpost hospital. The year was 1940, the government had just opened the area where our sawmill was located to settlers, and my parents, my grandparents, and an aunt and uncle were among that first small batch of Euro-Canadian settlers there. The place I was born into was wilderness, and we did not leave it until I was four years old, when we moved about fifteen miles to a hamlet where there was a school. We didn't leave that hamlet until I was six.

I have few really distinct memories of those years, but I remember the interior of our log house, I remember the Indian people in whose hunting territory we had unwittingly established ourselves, and I remember the bears and the roads, which were really just muddy trails hacked out of the bush by the settlers. I remember too the forest that was all around us, to me, at that time, a dark, brooding, and dangerous place into which we children never went. Yet I am sure that starting my life in such a place influenced me permanently. Nonetheless, for the rest of my childhood and adolescence, as we moved farther and farther south, until on my thirteenth birthday we arrived in the metropolis of Saskatoon (about fifty thousand people then), I convinced myself that I had been born for some not-clearly-defined glamorous life in the city, that the city was my natural home. Without being consciously aware that I had done so, I erased my wilderness childhood from my memory.

But, life being what it is, at thirty-six I arrived back in wilderness of a sort, that is, on a ranch in southwest Saskatchewan, only a few miles from the Montana border and a few more from—equally nowhere—southeastern Alberta. Now my home was the grasslands of North America. From our ranch, the nearest tree that no one had planted and watered was about eight and a half miles straight west. (Riding in a taxi in Los Angeles once I got great delight out of giving this answer to our driver, who had asked some polite question about where I came from, and was dismayed to find that my answer impressed him not in the least.)

Before my new marriage I had been teaching at the University of Saskatchewan while I worked on a postgraduate degree there. I was a divorcee, a single parent of an adolescent son, I had embraced feminism, and I had a circle of close women friends, as well as most of my family in the same city. The day I arrived as a new wife on the ranch, I left behind all of these things—career, family, friends, my accustomed milieu—and entered a world about which I knew nothing. It was a world based entirely on land, and on agriculture as the means of livelihood, with family ties—shared blood—an absolute basis of the society. I did not speak the "language" of the agricultural world, I knew no one, I had no relatives nearby, I couldn't even ride a horse.

The upshot of all this radical change, and the resulting immense psychic dislocation and loneliness, was that I began to go for walks on the prairie, the one thing I could do that required no special knowledge, or skills, or equipment, or even companions. I was fortunate that my husband's family's ranch consisted of thirteen thousand acres of grassland, only twelve hundred of which had ever been plowed, and even more fortunate in that I had married a man who cherished his many acres of grass and drastically understocked it (in animal-to-acres ratio) to keep a healthy and beautiful range: the grass abundant, the sage, greasewood, and cactus in an appropriate ratio to the grasses and other plants.

I walked every day that my health and the weather allowed. Very soon I stopped taking a sketchpad or a book with me and began simply to walk, to look, and to think about what I saw and heard around me. Mostly, though, I used the time to deal with my own burgeoning spiritual and psychological crisis, which had put me in such a state that before more than a couple of years had passed, had anyone asked, I could not have said who I was, or where my life might take me. Because of this crisis, I was full of questions to which I had no answers, and thus I was opened to the world around me—opened in that I did not have the solid boundaries of belief and emotion people have when they feel secure, centred, and in control of their lives.

Although so much of my new life was so unfamiliar to me that I felt myself to be floundering nearly all the time, in another way, my sense of familiarity with this way of life was growing. I began to remember my own, long-buried history: the corduroy roads, the howling of timber wolves, the constant sightings and fear of bears, and the northern lights shifting and moving palely in the twilight or night sky, the stars often visible through them. I was surrounded, as I had been through my early childhood, by Nature in her pure state. Once again I watched the moon as she waxed and waned across the sky; I rose with the sun; what I would do each day was once again determined by the season and the weather. The position of the hands on the clock no longer drove my life. I walked, and I thought, and sometimes I forgot to think at all, and simply was. During those moments when I was not buttoned snugly inside myself, the land itself found its way into me, and taught me.

My sense of there being something more on the land than grass, rocks, and sky began first with rare, powerful, and extraordinarily beautiful—if also bewilderingly enigmatic—dreams. In the first of these it was night and I was gazing out the back door of the old ranch house's porch at a dazzlingly beautiful eagle so huge that with its wings outspread as it soared above me, it covered the whole forty or so acres of the ranch yard. In front of me on the small cement square stood a six- or eight-foot-tall owl, and although differently coloured and marked, it was as stunningly beautiful as the eagle. I stood watching the eagle as it hovered above me, and I tried to keep out the owl, which seemed to be trying to get into the porch with me. In the dream neither was in the least threatening, and I was not afraid of either amazing, archetypal creature.

One does not simply dismiss such a dream, or ever forget it, and so part of my long journey in learning about nature was spurred by my intense desire to learn the meaning of my wonderful dreams. I began a voyage into my own psyche, too, which I pursued through books about psychology, mythology, feminist spirituality, and other, less easily categorized offshoots of these scholarly subjects, such as the psychology of religion and mysticism. I had begun to think that my intensified dreaming was related to my new life, lived, as it was, with only an outdoor toilet—so that, day or night, I constantly had to be going outside—and in a house that provided only the most minimal shield between us and the vast prairie wilderness that surrounded us. I understood my intensified dreaming as part of living in nature and as caused by this closeness to nature.

Not that I understood what this relationship—my dreaming and its connection to nature—consisted of. What struck me was the great beauty of nature, not in the sense of nature as landscape—although that was there too—but more as holder of some mysterious, universal meaning. But this idea remained unarticulated, not fully at the conscious level, and unexamined. My entire psyche was shifting and changing in a profound way, but I did not know where any of this change was leading and could not even begin to speculate about its outcome. And so I studied mythology, and feminist history, and the literature of psychotherapy.

The other major effect, though, of living so close to nature had to do with what happened to me during my waking hours. This began early in my marriage when one day, working quietly at my writing, alone at the kitchen table in the old ranch house, I felt an urge to go walking on the prairie. This urge was very powerful. I felt it deep inside me, deep in my gut, as I recall, and it seemed I had no choice but to give in to it. I believe this need or desire came from outside myself, because I remember finding it uncomfortably strong, and I blindly, with reluctance, obeyed it, going out and rushing across the nearby summerfallow field as if I had a destination, although I had no clear idea where I was going.

I reached the end of the field and crawled under the barbed wire fence onto the prairie, and after a moment of waiting, I turned and began to head south. I knew I was going in the "right" direction, but I did not know why it was the right direction, and I still had no idea what it was I was looking for, although that I was looking for something was now clear to me. One part of me was frightened and wanted only to go back to the safety of my kitchen, while another part wanted to give itself over entirely to this extraordinary experience.

For once, my adventurous side won out, and after further climbing and descent of grassy hills, I saw in the distance what I knew I'd been looking for. It was a glacial erratic made of mauve-tinted, creamy dolomite rock that rested near the bottom of a long, slowly ascending, flat-topped ridge. I went to the rock—I remember that I was running by this time—which was about six feet long, two and a half feet wide, and perhaps three feet high at its highest point. I examined it, admired it, and then began to walk slowly away from it up the ridge. As I walked, I began to find stone circles in the grass, altogether about a dozen of them of varying sizes, some of which were half-circles.

By this time, most of my confusion and fear had left me, and now I felt a strong sense of awe and gratitude to the force, whatever it was, that had led me out to find these structures nestled in the grass. When I reached the last one, I stepped inside it, feeling a strong need to acknowledge the miracle that had just overcome me. (How else was I to understand this? I didn't know why this had happened; I didn't know what the circles were; I didn't know why I should need to see them, or what the "force" was I had felt so compelled to obey that had brought me to them.) I tried to think how I might respond. After a moment, I turned and slowly, one by one, faced each of the four directions. And then, released from my compulsion, I turned and walked back to the house.

YEARS PASSED, MY PSYCHOLOGICAL crisis deepened and grew layers, I began to make progress in understanding myself and my life, but very slowly and painfully, sometimes rising to moments of joy, but just as often sinking to near despair. I continued my studies, I continued writing, and I began to publish novels and stories and to write plays. I continued to walk on the prairie, and such strange adventures as the one I have just disclosed continued to happen to me.

I will recount, very briefly, some of these experiences. Once, as I studied the prairie and the distant hillsides, my vision changed, and I began to do a particular kind of visual sweeping and yet focusing, a most powerful and utilitarian kind of looking—I believe, seeing the landscape as an experienced Aboriginal hunter might. Try as I might, I haven't been able to do it again.

Another time, studying an area of bush very hard, I felt my consciousness travelling out of me and moving across the grass by itself. As soon as I noticed this was happening, it stopped.

And another time I was stomping across the grass in a fury over something I can't remember now, and I tripped and fell headlong into a bed of sage, which buoyed me up, and as I lay there, I felt the anger drain out of me and gradually be replaced by a wave of relaxation and peace. But as I fell, I saw a group of Amerindian women dressed as the women of my bush childhood had been, in long, dark cotton dresses and head scarves, packed tightly together, laughing at me.

I found things too, sometimes things that were there one day but that on subsequent walks I could never find again. One of these findings, most notably, was a polished white quartz rod about six inches long and a white quartz sphere perhaps two inches in diameter. To this day I can only guess what made me put back on the ground so startling a find and walk away from it. I did mark carefully in my mind where I had put these objects, but even though I spent days searching (and continue to look to this day) I have never seen them again.

Another day, I found a large chert rock, about the size of a foot-stool. Its rough brown sides had been broken cleanly off to expose its bluish-grey interior, as if someone had hit it, just so, hard, with (I suppose) another rock, in order to break off large chunks from each of its sides. It looked as if this had just been done yesterday, and I was very excited by this find, because Plains people often used chert to make tools and points. Now I had found a source-rock. But the next time I went looking for the rock, I found that the sharp edges, the clean, shiny faces of the cleavage that I remembered seeing, had become rough, aged, spotted with at least hundred-year growths of lichen.

I began to think, *I am being shown things. I am being taught.*

I was filled with awe, both for what seemed to me to be a great gift, of which I felt myself unworthy, and because I now knew beyond doubt that another, unseen world exists, that its denizens—whoever or whatever they might be—could communicate with humans if they chose. And I wondered why I was being shown all of this, for what purpose.

I was a Euro-Canadian, raised a Christian, and a rational, edu-cated woman. I did not fully understand that there was any other vantage point from which to view the world. I knew, of course, that such viewpoints existed, but I had never paid them any attention. I had, however, long since expanded my reading to include the history and spiritual systems of the Plains Amerindian people, and I was finding that my reading, my visions (or whatever they were), my dreams, and my archaeological finds were all meshing to teach me a new spiritual worldview. The result was that I was becoming steeped in this new spirituality.

It was the strangest thing! Of course I worried sometimes that I was losing my mind, but mostly what I was learning seemed so absolutely right that I couldn't question it. Besides that, because I wasn't telling anybody, I didn't have to deal with anybody's skepticism or denial. I vowed to go wherever these astonishing experiences were taking me, to follow them as far as they desired me to go, even if they led to my death—and they still might—because I felt privileged, and humbled that all of this might happen to me, and as curious, too, as any insatiable scientist about what it all meant.

But from the moment of my first strange calling out onto the prairie, and my deep search within myself for an appropriate response to it, resulting in my turning to face each of the four directions in stillness and awe, I had begun to understand that land—nature—was more than the merely physical. I saw that it had a consciousness of some kind, an overarching meaning, or something I finally called *presence*. And I did not know what that *presence* was. I thought then that nature must be alive, and real, and full of knowledge, or perhaps wisdom. In my first nonfiction book I capitalized the word *Nature*, as Thoreau had done. And, further, I had begun to think that my experiences in nature must have been given to me by Nature her/him/itself. That the *presence* I have mentioned was, in fact, Nature as a living being.

If this were true—and there was no one around me to insist that it was not—if I were right about that "force" that had called me out onto the prairie that day years earlier, then I had better find a way to behave on the land that would demonstrate my new understanding.

I had better not fail to show my respect to the land. I began to search for ways to demonstrate this respect and settled on a few that grew out of the particular kind of landscape in which I lived: I stopped picking wildflowers, although I studied them closely and admired them; I stopped walking on rocks or even sitting on them, and if I picked up a small one to examine it, I put it back exactly in the place and alignment in which I had found it. I no longer took away culturally modified stones—scrapers or flakes left from tool or weapon making—but left them where they were. And I never entered the fields, or left them, without offering thanks for the privilege to this disembodied *presence*, which I felt so strongly and with which I dreamt of making a more solid kind of contact.

To do this last, I practised not-thinking on my walks, letting myself fully appreciate my surroundings, giving myself over to the place in which I found myself. I tried to keep myself open to whatever might happen, to whatever might come to me. I tried also to be more than appreciative of the beauty I found on the prairie. I felt that all of these measures, although each fairly trivial in itself, were a way of demonstrating to that unseen *presence* or *presences* that I was beginning to understand as Nature that I had accepted it for what it was.

At first, of course, this was such an astonishing discovery that I spent all my thought on trying simply to grasp it and then in probing its texture and its boundaries. I had, since I was about fifteen, been struggling with my faith. (I'd been raised as an old-fashioned Roman Catholic, although my mother had not been Catholic and, I believe, came to detest Catholicism. The legacy of this was pain and confusion in spiritual matters for her children.) At eighteen I declared there was no God, and lived with that belief until the extended spiritual crisis that began in my late thirties, when I began to read widely and deeply in spiritual literature and to have what can only be named spiritual experiences. And then to realize I had always had spiritual experiences, going back into my childhood.

But the God of my childhood—that fierce old man in the sky— was gone forever; dogma, theology—all were gone, vanished, utterly refused by my new understanding of the world. As I struggled and searched and dreamt and walked in the fields and read more books, I became sure that no existing belief system would ever work for me in its entirety; I would have to slowly, painfully, twig by tiny twig, build my own spiritual home, and that was very painful to me and sometimes frightened me and caused me to despair.

I found, though, that I couldn't fully commit myself to this idea of Nature as a disembodied being. Now, wondering if I were right in thinking that Nature was all-powerful, I wondered also what this notion did to my conception of God, or something I thought of more as "God-ness." Did this mean that Nature was God? I was not ready to embrace pantheism, and I held that thought in abeyance for a time down the road when I would know more.

Very late in the game, not that long ago, I learned that the Plains people, at least traditionally, had a very different hierarchy of being from that of Christians (or semi-Christians, as I was); I don't know how extensive this hierarchy is throughout the Aboriginal world. Aboriginal people too place the Creator above all parts of creation, but Mother Earth comes next, and (or so I've read) she is followed by the Sun, Moon, Stars, and Plants, then by Small Life, then the Winged and the Aquatic, then two- to four-legged animals, and last of all, by Human Beings.

Most Christians would read this and then, with an astonished smile, dismiss it. But now I read it with delight because it helped to make sense of my experiences—or my experiences made more sense in the light of this information. But still, I couldn't help but think that the ability to think, to ponder, to create, and to invent put humans in a different order from the rest of creation.

Often, in my continuing search, I would remember that dream—or vision—I had had when I was a very young woman and a new mother: How the universe was itself benign and serene and how everything in it—sky, grass, trees, and humans—was made of the same material, a material that I thought was perhaps itself a kind of consciousness. I began to ponder it once again, but with more seriousness, and with my knowledge from my years of reading to inform me. But, nearly forty years after I had had the vision, I still could not find a way to make what I had seen work as part of my daily life, and I continued to try to delve below the dream's images or to re-pattern them, to find the *real* meaning, the one that would sustain me for the rest of my time on earth. But I could not.

ABOUT THE SAME TIME, I HAD begun to realize that the field to which I devoted my book *Wild Stone Heart*, and in which I had walked for twenty years, was an Amerindian graveyard. I was shocked to think that it had taken me nearly twenty years to *see* this and that no other Euro-Canadian either, as far as I knew, had recognized—had they even seen them?—the lichen-covered, half-buried stone cairns lying throughout the field for the graves that they were.

I didn't know who the people buried there were, or when they had died and been buried, or how they had died: In battle? From smallpox? Perhaps by starvation? And were they Siksika? Plains Cree? Nakota? Gros Ventres? Or had they died long before any of these names and tribal affiliations had come into existence? I grieved for those dead people—so many dead—and that there were none of their people to mourn them, or to say prayers over their bones.

My original explanation of the "communications" had been that they must be from Nature itself, an idea I had never wholeheartedly accepted. Now I began to see that nearly all of these incidents had been associated with the past, specifically with that of the original inhabitants, the Aboriginal people of this area of the Great Plains. Nearly all of them, come to think of it, had had to do with stone circles, with chert flakes and tools, with buffalo drive lines and hearths, and even with what turned out to be a turtle effigy.

And then I also, slowly, dubiously at first, and then with more certainty, began to see that the communications—if I might call them that—I had received had come not from a presence I had considered might be Nature herself but, instead, from the souls of the dead. I knew that Amerindian people would say that they had come from the Ancestors, who in traditional belief systems remain a continuing source of wisdom and of not-inconsiderable power. And I remembered reading the American poet Gary Snyder quoting a Crow elder he'd heard speak at a conference somewhere in the American West. The elder had said that he believed that the old powers were still present in the land and might speak—even to White people—if those people stayed long enough on a piece of land and were attentive enough to it. This realization was a great shock to me, and at first it frightened me a little. But I stopped thinking about the souls of the dead and began to think about the Ancestors—not mine, but those of the Aboriginal people who had, for thousands of years before the arrival of Euro-Canadians, made all of the Great Plains their home— and I lost most of my fear.

I had been plunked down in the middle of the Aboriginal worldview, and I looked around at the grass and the stones and the sky and did not know what to do. Spend the rest of my life sitting on the spiritual fence? Go out and buy myself a drum and a feathered headdress? But I had been in one sweat lodge and had run out (to my shame) because I could not give myself over to it: I did not want the visions I knew would come; I thought I would suffocate, and I was terrified. Now I kept repeating to myself: I am a modern woman, I am educated, I love theatre, opera, books. I am not an Indian. I am not an Indian.

IN ALL MY YEARS OF internal struggle to make sense of the world and of my own life, there had been one final lesson: I must not rely on what I read was the correct thing to think or do, or on what people told me was right, but instead, I must base my decisions about life and how to live it on my own experience and my own ideas about that experience. I kept repeating to myself this one, firm conviction by which I had made such spiritual progress as I could claim. In the light of this dictum, I returned once again to the magnificent vision I had had when I was twenty-three: the primeval, archetypal vision about the oneness of the universe. That vision (although I'd learned it was pretty small potatoes in the world of mysticism) had been the highest spiritual experience I had had in my life, the most complete revelation about existence.

One day, thirty-seven years after I had had that vision, at the age of sixty, I realized that my long search for its meaning had occurred simply because I couldn't accept that the dream meant what it said— that everything in creation was made of the same material, that the Christian hierarchy, with humans placed just below God, was, quite simply, wrong. This meaning was so alien to everything I'd been raised to believe that I hadn't been able to accept it and had spent all those long years searching for a meaning that I was sure was there, but hidden below its misleading surface. Then I realized that I could now *see* this elemental fact, because of my reading, yes, but mostly because of my strange, mystical experiences on the prairie.

Then, with a tremendous shock, it finally came to me that the spiritual world of the Aboriginal people of the Great Plains—as well as I understood it—meshed with the vision that had dogged me ever since I'd had it when I was that young mother, overworked, fearful, and blind, but full of dreams of glory.

I AM STILL TRYING TO SEE how such a belief system might work for a modern, urbanized, Euro-Canadian woman like me. But almost six years ago my husband and I helped the Nature Conservancy of Canada turn the Butala ranch into the Old Man on His Back* Prairie and Heritage Conservation Area, and this year we are placing the field of *Wild Stone Heart*—the field full of Aboriginal graves—under a conservation easement that will protect it in perpetuity, and we continue to work with environmental agencies to help preserve what little native grassland is left. This is all very well and good, as the saying goes.

But speaking in an intimately personal way, I confess that mostly I am still sitting on the spiritual fence, the "heresy" of pantheism, on my practical days, still scaring me, yet, on my fully "open" days, the unconditional truth of mystical vision erasing all doubt.

---

* The plateau on which the ranch sits is called "Old Man on His Back," an Aboriginal name which, for once, stuck.

RICK BASS

A Texas Childhood

RICK BASS *is the author of eighteen books of fiction and nonfiction, including* The Hermit's Story *and* The Roadless Yaak. *He lives with his family in northwest Montana's Yaak Valley, where there is still not a single acre of designated wilderness.*

IT'S LATE JANUARY, AND I'M sitting on the porch of my parents' farm in south Texas, watching our daughters, nine and six, playing in the middle of a pasture, surrounded by balmy breezes and birdsong—a week's respite from the Montana winter. After a long winter's accruing numbness, this premature burst of song, and of warmth, rests exquisitely upon our skin.

Watching the girls play, so far from the Montana wilderness, I find myself wondering, What, from childhood, informs us as adults? What images of nature—and what relationships—last? The physical memories of the world, surely, and yet also the fabric of stories. Both must make a child, and then an adult.

It seems a paradox to me that the more deeply the physical senses are engaged, the more deeply the mind can be stirred: as if birdsong, breeze-stir, sunlight in winter, distant dog-bark, reminding me of my own childhood in Texas, are but story themselves, occurring again and again, and in that manner, they are as strong in one's mind as they ever were in the original physical sensation.

For a long time, I thought the physical senses and the life of the mind were oppositional, as if the two were engaged eternally in some giant tag-team pro-wrestling match of winner-take-all. Like so many

others, I fell into the trap of thinking we were separate from nature
—that we had not been birthed from the dust, and that because of
the size and complexity of our brains, we were the exception to any
rule we desired.

But now I have come to think that the mind and the physical
senses are both a form of story, which I would define as little more
than the electrical charge that exists—like sparks across a synapse—
between touch and the processing of information gathered from that
touch, on its way into the catalogue of memory. If this is so, then
everything is story—everything living, at any rate, and much that is
not—and therefore, for a writer or storyteller, there could never be a
dearth of stories, only a dearth of time in which to tell them.

These tiles beneath my bare feet, my bare feet in January, for
instance—I aim to spend but a sentence or two on them, though
even as I sit here watching our girls play in the cow pasture (sitting
on beach towels in lawn chairs out in the bright sun in caps and sunglasses and swimsuits, as if they are at the ocean), I am reminded,
sparklike, of the story, the saga, of how these tiles beneath my feet
got here.

My parents, accompanied by my youngest brother, B. J., had
driven down to Mexico to buy the tiles more cheaply at the factory,
choosing from the culls that had never been shipped to various
ports—tiles of varying shades of salmon, tangerine, and sandstone-
red, tiles with little cat-and-dog-and-rooster-tracks on them, where
various domestic pets had scampered across the damp clay of the
still-drying tiles, after they were poured but before they were baked
in the kiln. A penny a tile, or some-such.

All right, five or six or seven sentences.

They'd taken their old manure-speckled, slick-tired cattle truck across the border, rather than renting a flatbed, and had stacked it full-to-groaning with tiles. In the summer heat, and on the ragged roads, they'd had various flat tires, so they kept having to offload all those tiles, one by one, to change each flat tire.

When they finally got to customs, my father was in a vile mood. Understandably, his trailer was pulled over to the special inspection line, where, after an hour or two of inching forward in the long line, it was finally examined, and he was told that it did not have proper inspection, that it would need to be quarantined, and that the manure he had brought into the country would have to be sprayed off and the trailer disinfected. He'd have to wait until Monday or maybe even Thursday of next week to get a permit—it was a Friday afternoon—unless he could produce some form of documentation—perhaps the Andrew Jackson or even the Ben Franklin kind.

The sagging trailer, with all its tonnage, was blocking the only lane through the customs-search line. One of the old bald-patched tires was hissing, as was the radiator. Another offloading was imminent. The cars and trucks in line behind my father seemed to stretch to the horizon, like the scales of some glittering reptile. Horns were honking.

"All right," my father said, handing the custom agent the keys. "You can have it. It's yours. I've had enough. Come on," he said to my mother and my brother, "we'll walk across. I'm tired of it. I don't want the tiles anymore, or the truck, or the trailer. We'll just leave it all here."

Steam was spewing from beneath the hood now, and the radiator was singing like a teakettle.

"*Wait*," the agent said, panicking now, refusing the keys. "Just go on."

They proceeded. It took another eight hours, and four more flat tires, but they finally got back home and eventually built their house and laid their tiles—and now B. J., who accompanied them on that sojourn at the tender age of seven, is twenty-nine, and a stonemason, comfortable and accomplished in the patient and rigorous discipline of stacking and unstacking, sorting and choosing and weighing and measuring—but that is another story. There can never be an end of stories; they travel in all directions, for all distances . . .

Which ones become the quarrystone below? Who knows what moments—what complications of the physical and the mental—of landscape and story—conspire to ignite the sparks of enduring memory, formative or pivotal or living memories?

What is the effect of various landscapes upon such memories?

WHERE WE LIVE NOW, the girls and Elizabeth and I, is deep in the forest on the edge of Canada, not Mexico. I believe that there are lightning-spark transformative moments in our lives, epiphanies, in which the milieu of all of one's previous experience is illuminated into an Event, an experience more profound somehow than even memory itself, so that the event seems to have somehow always been within you, waiting only to occur, predestined, miraculous, and splendidly unique, and yet in retrospect completely unavoidable.

Perhaps there are a handful of such deep upwelling moments, or events, in every life—and yet (as if with the patience of a stone-mason) I want deeply to believe that the general background daili-ness of one's life is as important, in the long run, as any of those handful of defining moments that provide the sudden jolt of deeper awareness or even understanding.

WHAT INSPIRATIONS AND UNDERSTANDINGS will come from the fabric of the elements we have chosen to make available to our daughters? How will their lives and interiors be shaped—not formed, but shaped—by their seeing, in all the days of their childhood, these mountains and their storms, these moose and wolves and eagles and bears? By helping me hunt and take and then give thanks for and then clean and prepare our own meals from the forest—deer and elk and fish and mushrooms and berries?

How will it all add up for them—the day the wolf was in the yard, the day the mountain lion followed us while skiing, the day the golden eagle caught the goose in the marsh?

What is the sum of this daily appreciating, and even becoming accustomed to these things—not taking them for granted, but becoming accustomed to them—until you become so comfortable with the shape of things that their presence in your life fits you like your own skin?

And further, do the occasional childhood upwellings of grace—characterized chiefly by a sudden sense of profound *belongingness* and the witnessing of extreme beauty—manifest themselves differently for woods children already accustomed to being surrounded by such beauty? Do moments of deep nature-epiphany really arrive only for children of the suburbs and the inner cities?

Maybe a slow and steady braid of beauty is every bit as durable and powerful—perhaps even more so—as any tiny cluster, or bouquet, of crucible-forged revelations. Perhaps in the end, it's all the same, and there's little difference, in this regard, between a Houston suburb and a Montana wilderness.

I don't believe that, however. I believe it is more a testament to the incredible strength and purity of the hearts of children that the epiphanies of the natural world's beauty can and will come almost anywhere, at any time, rising as if from below, unsummoned.

I think also that such a phenomenon makes the presence of wilderness all the more important, not less.

If semi-urban or domesticated nature can exert such profound change and power upon us, then what mystery must reside and flourish in the seething woods and swamps and mountains that lie beyond the reach of our roads?

If such glimpses of grace and revelation can be seen by children in even the narrowest, vanishing wedges of semi-domesticated nature, then what store of tenderness must lie at the source, or the headwaters—available in such a free and undiluted state as to perhaps be readily observed, and deeply felt, by even the jaded eyes and hardening hearts of adults?

I GREW UP IN THE SUBURBS of Houston—at the edge of the suburbs, the farthest suburb at the time, at the edge of the Katy prairie, in the ribbon of hardwood forest that laced the edges of Buffalo Bayou.

There was a farthermost place I could get to by riding my bike down sandy trails for a mile or so, beyond the last road, and beyond the last house, and then by travelling farther on foot, through greenbriar and cane and willow and dewberry, along the game trails that followed the high cutbank bluffs of the serpentine bayou, travelling several miles of bayou-bend oxbow to traverse a single mile on the map. It was a physical engagement that impressed itself upon my way of thinking, even my way of sentence-making, and is still where I am most comfortable.

There was always something to see, and I didn't want to miss anything. Leopard frogs leaping from bluffs into the muddy current below; giant soft-shelled turtles floating camouflaged in sun-dappled patches of bayou, their dinosaur necks seeming as long as those of snakes; primitive alligator gars longer than I was tall and as thick around as my waist, cruising on the surface like mysterious submarines; armadillos, again seeming as strange as dinosaurs and more beautiful than any bronze or golden jewellery, slithering across the trail, alarmed by my approach; and box turtles wandering through the forest; and flying squirrels, fox squirrels, gray squirrels, raccoons, and opossums scurrying up the trees . . . Nine-lined skunks scampered across and beneath the dry leaves of oak and hickory, their tiny scrabbly sounds like the first few faint drops of rain upon those same leaves . . .

There were sometimes even deer, there at the edge of the bayou—what a shock it was to encounter an animal larger than me—and often, while I was running down one of those trails, running for the joy of being alive and running, and with the wind in my face, I would sometimes surprise deer coming down those same trails; and in their fright, they would sometimes crash through the brush and hurtle down those steep banks and dive into the bayou and begin swimming for the other side.

There was a lake back in those woods—a deep swamp, really, already in the first stages of eutrophication, but all the richer for it— which I called Hidden Lake, for the fact that I never encountered anyone else there, or even a sign of anyone's presence—no stumps, no litter, not even any footprints—as well as for the manner in which one came to the lake: passing through an old-growth forest of pine and hardwoods, with no indication that the lake lay before you, until you stumbled right onto it, the many grey-spar rotting hulks of dead trees that surrounded its blackwater reflection forming roosts for an aviary that was nothing less than astounding.

Great blue herons, seemingly as large as pterodactyls, would croak their ancient cries and leap into the sky—sometimes in their haste the old rotten limb they'd been perching on would fall into the lake with a large splash—and wood ducks, which back then had been hunted almost to extinction, would leap from those same black waters in a spray and blur, squeaking their whistly alarm cries.

Best of all were the egrets—snowy egrets, as well as the cattle egrets: ghostly birds rising and flying through the forest, as brilliantly white as the water beneath them was black, their slow, graceful departure mirrored perfectly in the still waters beneath them . . .

I went there almost every day after I got home from school—I suppose this would have been over thirty years ago now—until the roads began being built into it—bulldozers and chain saws and concrete trucks, and fluttering ribbons tied to trees that I knew individually. And just like that, over the course of only a season or two, the woods were filled with noise, and then they vanished.

I was moving into adolescence, by that time, and probably would have had my attention diverted anyway, for a while—and in that regard, I never really had to grieve that loss, as I had begun to supplant it, even as the forest was being levelled and the swamp being drained. It could have been a lot more painful than it was.

It is clear to me only now, in the writing of this memory, that what was most valuable in those sojourns, beyond the direct exposure to wildlife in its native habitat, was the complete absence of knowledge, while in the lake's presence, that that habitat would not last forever—that in fact it was already doomed, even as I was run-

ning through those woods. I completely lacked what Wendell Berry
has called "the forethought of grief."

And perhaps an even larger blessing was my failure to realize, for
a long time, that I was part-and-parcel of that taking: that my weight-
upon-the-earth was part of the very thing that was flushing those
copperheads and box turtles from hiding and sending those deer
crashing into the bayou, swimming for the other side, to the brief
safety of the wilder country beyond.

It is the unoriginal and damning realization of the fact of my
complicity—of all of our complicity—that has helped lead me into
activism: a response fuelled really by nothing more complex than an
awestruck love of, and reverence for, wild creation, mixed with what
remains perhaps a child's naive and deeply felt sense of justice and
injustice.

THOSE DAYS, I BELIEVE, WERE for me the braid, rather than
the epiphany: the slow accruing weave that helped form a medium
out of which future lightning-bolt moments could occur. Days in
which I became more fluent in the language of that which would
speak more clearly to me, and had already been speaking to me, and
would speak to me again and again.

I don't think any sort of woods-fluency is requisite for illuminating or defining moments to occur—I think these illuminations or
epiphanies of beauty are a universal phenomenon, in which the
beauty of the natural world, and the grace of our inclusion in it, is
shown to us as surely as if drapes or curtains have been peeled back
or blinders lifted from our eyes. I suspect that there are periods in our
lives when we are susceptible to such moments, or sufficiently undis-
tracted to refocus upon the world and see deeper into its beauty. And

whether these moments result from some cellular activity within us, some maturation or shifting hormonal processes, some new-forming variance in the profile of our blood chemistry, or whether these moments—these shining moments—are dispensed to us from above every few years, as if from some great and largely impersonal cog-and-gear revolution of stars and time and chance and fate, I have no idea: I know only that they exist.

Whatever the reason for such epiphanies, I'm grateful that they exist in domesticated nature; and in the rawer, farther wilderness, too.

GROWING UP IN THE SUBURBS, I milked whatever wilderness I could from the faint patterings of creatures beneath the leaves and from the high-above brayings of the great migrating flocks of geese, always synonymous with weather changes, and from little more than the north winds themselves, which, though rare, would clear out most of the petrochemical haze that hung over the city like a glowing dome. I milked wilderness as much from the ghosts of wildness-gone-by, or from the imagination, as from any remnant essence of the thing.

Perhaps instinctively, I looked north, five hours north and west, to the place where my family had gone deer hunting each year since the 1930s. The place we called the deer pasture was up in the hill country and seemed infinitely wilder than did the prairie around Houston, as the prairie was being devoured by the swelling population, the boom of which I was but one, and devoured too by the first breezy ticklings of nonstop run-and-gun affluence.

Hunted for all the decades previous by my grandfather, father, uncle, and cousins, the deer pasture was for me a hardscrabble land of granite domes and prickly pear, scorpions and rattlesnakes, where ghosts seemed even less distant: a place where fragments of arrowheads could still be found, as could the remains of homesteaders' cabins, far back in the clutches of the encroaching juniper, at the edges of vanishing seeps and springs. It was a place steeped in story and even myth, which converged with a biological richness.

Just across the upthrown side of the Balcones Escarpment, a geological uplift that separates ecotones as distinctly as did the parting of any sea (square in the midst of a buckled igneous zone that geologists call the Central Texas Mineral Uplift), the deer pasture was home to not just deer and turkeys, but to foxes, bobcats, coyotes, and even the rumours of mountain lions. Our family went there to camp, also, and to see the flowers in spring and to picnic in summer, and because it was such a long drive from Houston—longer still, in those days of rougher roads—we usually arrived late at night, having left after my father got off work on a Friday evening.

We crossed the cattle guard and drove in on the caliche road, I would wake up and look out the front windshield to see jackrabbits and cottontails racing down the shining white ribbon of road in front of us, eyes red-ablaze in the headlights' illumination, raising puffs of white dust with each acrobatic leap. Getting out to open the gate, I would always be struck, almost overwhelmed, by the brightness of the stars, by the cleaner scent of the woods around me, and by both the silence and the sounds that helped define or bound the silence: the frogs and crickets, owls and coyotes. The big sweet nothing. Even then, it aroused in me a feeling of calm, great peace, and even now, after having seen far greater wilderness, it still does.

I PREFER THE SLOW and enduring form of sculpting—a geological sort of pace that allows for rises and falls, mistakes and redemptions both, but with absolution, and success, in the end; a pace in which any and all clumsiness yields finally to grace, as if that clumsiness has metamorphosed, transformed by time running across and around that clumsiness like a river running across a rock mid-river, polishing it to some elegant, fitted shape. It doesn't matter, does it, whether you get your hundred volts one day at a time, a volt each day, or all at once?

Often even a single volt of the world's beauty, the world's wonder, feels to me like a hundred. I am drawn more toward the daily, understated devotional of staring out at a marsh for long moments at a time, or at a forested, uncut mountainside, than toward any search for high-intensity moments of illumination, simply because I'm not sure the husk of my body could hold up to the rigours of any amped-up intensities, so sweet and total are the pleasures of even those single volts.

My girls are far flashier in the world—far more fitted to it, already: bright and beautiful and certainly deeply loved. What will their moments be? Which will influence them more strongly—the slow daily braid, the continuum of nature, or the curtain-parting moments of supreme revelation? It can't be controlled, of course, or perhaps even observed, not even by them. Of my own defining moments in nature, only rarely do I ever remember being aware in-the-moment of thoughts as clichéd as *I will never forget this*, or, *Wow, this is a revelation*. Even those highly illuminated moments sank deep, as if into the river of my life, unrealized at first, and it was only after I had gone on some distance past them that I understood in retrospect that that's what had happened: that they were foundational images, the emplacement of mid-river boulders that somehow changed the patterns of all the subsequent flow downstream.

The moments cannot be set up in advance. Magic comes when it comes. Perhaps this is another reason I tend toward, or am more comfortable with, the accumulated daily sweetness over the exalted once- or twice- or thrice-in-a-lifetime euphorias. I can help provide for, or lead the girls to, those quieter places. No one can do magic, but any of us can show up for work each day, can lead children to the raw materials that, once braided, conduct that magic. Like apprentice workers pushing a wheelbarrow full of various quarrystones to the place where a master stonemason is working, we can gather and select and then ferry those individual days.

Beyond that, nothing—only magic. The labourers can only show up for work each day.

THE OTHER DAY, I HAD NOT been thinking of these things—the illuminating moments of childhood—when one seemed to occur for my younger daughter, Lowry, and me, not upwelling from the buried humus of centuries below or from the braid-and-twine of the blood within us, but embracing us instead like fog, like a single layer of cloud whose slow-drifting path (the fog-cloud migrating slowly, in the manner of an animal moving through the woods—a moose, perhaps, or a bear) intersected, that day, with our own curious wanderings.

It was a rainy day in January, cold and raw, ragged and dark. The old snow already down was the only light in the world, and even it was dull. The moss hanging from the trees was sodden, and it was one of those days when dusk seemed determined to arrive two hours early.

The girls were home from school and were hanging out on the couch, eating slices of apples and slices of cheese, watching some movie on video—*The Princess Diaries*, or something like that. I can't remember how it happened. Mary Katherine might have discovered she had some homework to do, but Lowry and I ended up going out-side to ski for a while. I have to confess, I kind of forced the issue—something about the comfort with which they were ensconced alarmed me, the fact that they had not been outside all day, and that dusk was coming on—and there might have been a little of my own winter-craziness, stir-craziness, at play too, for I ended up issuing a mandate, a proclamation, acknowledging to Lowry that while yes, I understood she didn't want to go outside, didn't want to ski, it was going to be a requirement, this rainy day, that we go outside for a moment, even if only fifty yards up the driveway. That it was for our health, and to break the braid, the pattern, of the couch.

I don't know why I felt we had to get out that one afternoon. Certainly, other days have passed—rainy, foggy, drizzly days in the winter—in which none of us venture outside.

But this nearing-dusk day I was agitated. It didn't seem that I was asking too much. "Fifty yards," I told her. "I know that you don't want to go outside today. We'll come right back in. But we have to go fifty yards up the driveway. We just have to get out for a minute or two. We don't even have to have fun," I said. "Think of it as work—like emptying the cat litter, or something."

Maybe this was shaping up to be a train wreck. *Cat litter* equals the *great outdoors?* What surer way to dull a child's innate curiosity and even enthusiasm for the natural world? Had I snapped, in the seasonal deprivation of light, and turned into one of those awful eco-fascist parents? How was this dictum any different, really, to a six-year-old, from forced wind sprints or a hundred pushups? Dad the drill sergeant.

I'll tell you the truth—there were a few tears as Lowry got up and turned the movie off and then pulled on her snow pants and laced up her cross-country ski boots. "Why do we have to go fifty yards?" she asked—a valid question—to which I answered, "We just do."

Maybe I was feeling something after all. Some summons. Or not. What does it matter?

Lowry stamped outside. She can be more obstinate than a mule. She can be more obstinate than me. *Why*, she asked again, and now that I had her outside, into raw nature this nasty, foggy day—now that we had somehow broken the cycle of the couch, where, now that I remember, she had spent the previous afternoon, also—I had achieved what I wanted—I was able to negotiate downward, and said, "Okay, you don't have to ski fifty yards; I'll pull you in the sled for fifty yards."

She dug in further, sulked deeper. She's not one to negotiate. Give her any weakness and she moves away from it, not toward it. Was I going to have to physically lift her into the sled? "Oh, *wah*," I said, "please, Daddy, don't pull me around in the sled, please don't make Princess ride in the sleigh, oh, *wah*." For a moment she started to giggle—it was enough for me to lift her in—but then she folded her arms and the Great Lip came back out.

"*I don't want to go*," she growled. I felt that I had gone too far and yet that I had made too much of it to back down. The child-rearing books, I knew, would have all sorts of lucid and correct advice, but that didn't do me any good, for Lowry was already in the sled.

We started up the driveway, into the gloom. I pointed out the fifty-yard mark. She pouted and griped the whole way, milking her full fifty yards' worth. My God, how I hope she ends up on our side; how formidable an adversary she would be on the other side.

At the fifty-yard mark, I turned around, true to my word, and began running down the steep hill. That broke the ice-shell, the plaster cast of displeasure, and as she laughed and then asked me to do it again, I felt like an alchemist or magician.

It was the most amazing feeling: as if I had been holding her unhappiness cupped in both of my hands and had done some trick— rolled it around for a moment as if mixing dust and water to make clay—and when I opened my hands again, there was happiness where previously had existed only unhappiness.

It wasn't me, of course. It was the woods and the earth—the slope of the hill, the laws of gravity, and so forth—and the condition of childhood, which seeks joy so earnestly and relentlessly—but it was wonderful nonetheless to be witnessing it and participating in it.

I pulled her a few more times, and then—raging hypocrite!—I began to long for the warmth of the wood stove, the winter cabin light of hearth and home. Lowry was all bundled up, but I had neither coat nor gloves, having been certain we would travel only fifty yards.

Each time I suggested that we head back inside, she coaxed me into one more run. But then, finally, when we truly had made the last run, the one-more after the one-more after the one-more after the one-more—rather than going inside to warm up (*hot chocolate*, I urged her, and *Harry Potter*), she became absorbed by the myriad of deer tracks stippling the snow in the driveway: the regular herd of half a dozen (twenty-four hoofs) that wanders down the driveway at various times of the day.

There were tracks everywhere, travelling in all directions—days and days of tracks—but Lowry, with her typical singularity of focus, seized upon one track among all the hundreds of others and began following it, hunched over like Inspector Clousseau.

As best as I could tell, she stayed with it too, parsing out for a lit- tle while that one deer's tracks among so many others, identifying it by size and shape as well as smoking-gun freshness, the blue-glaze sheen of that one set of tracks among dozens possessing a slightly brighter glow. But soon enough, she was tracking in a wandering maze of tight little circles, a kaleidoscope of trailing, with me behind her, so that seen from above, our path would have resembled that of those little teacup-rides in amusement parks.

It was nearly full dusk now, and darker still, farther into the woods; and again, now that my mission was accomplished, I kept wanting to quit and to go back to the house and warm up—to call it a day—even as Lowry was growing more and more engaged in following those tracks.

What it felt like to me was that something around her was unspooling—that if I had had her on some sort of psychic leash, it suddenly no longer applied, for whatever reasons—and so I followed behind her and was careful not to comment or correct her, letting her believe instead that she was hot on the trail of that deer, stalking it inch by inch and foot by foot, and that we might come upon it at any moment. So lost was she in following the one set of tracks through the maze—travelling in slowly widening circles—that I felt certain she had lost track of time and was so totally into the tracking that in her mind we had travelled miles, rather than continuing to circle back to more or less the same starting point.

Eventually, however, the circles widened enough that we found ourselves coming nearer the marsh, and as if still believing she was following the same deer (and perhaps at any given moment she was), Lowry left off her circling style of tracking and began following the tracks in a line, like an eager hunter closing in, having solved the riddle and the challenge.

The deer—still one among dozens or hundreds—travelled,

according to Lowry, down toward my writing cabin and circled it before heading off farther into the woods, with so little light remaining now.

Do I know for certain that Lowry was betranced—illuminated—during this strange trailing, this impromptu, wandersome exploration? Not at all. And even during the travelling, the thought had not yet occurred to me. It was only when we heard the eerie whooping dusk cry of a pileated woodpecker, and she took my hand and led me to a clump of winter-bare alder, and hunkered down into a hiding position, that I began to consider that she was deeply in another world—or rather, deeply in this one.

"If we hide," she said, crouching behind a slender tree, "maybe he won't see us. Maybe he'll come closer."

The woodpecker called again, from high above, and not very far away, and Lowry pressed herself in closer against the spindly little alder, and motioned for me to hide myself better.

We watched intently, waiting for the woodpecker to show itself. I could feel Lowry's focus, patient and keen, and I marvelled at the purity of her desire. She didn't want to trap or hunt the bird, or even sneak up on it: she just wanted to see it, and to watch it, unobserved.

There was no way we could hide sufficiently behind that bare little alder, but Lowry didn't know that, or didn't believe it, and we waited longer, watching and listening. It was only when we finally heard the bird call again from much farther away and noted a deeper dimness—almost, but not quite yet, true dark—that we rose from our crouch and began walking back up the trail toward the house, with Lowry leading the way, excited and fulfilled, with the tears of less than an hour ago completely vanquished.

So strange was the turnaround in her mood and demeanour

that I wondered if the woods-euphoria hadn't somehow been set up by the chemistry of the tears, allowing her to feel the day more sharply.

Goofy thoughts, I know. But she seemed so self-assured, curious and confident both, that I couldn't help but wonder if the images of the day weren't etching themselves indelibly upon her, like light coming through a brief lens opening to expose itself to the waiting film within.

There's no way to tell, of course, other than to one day ask her, far into the future—to see if that memory has withstood the test of time—and it may be that she won't remember at all: that the moment was not for her the vertical illumination of light that I imagined I was witnessing but instead simply more of the "regular" daily braid of her life; that the moment was not a landmark pivot-point, a boulder emplaced in the centre of the river's current, forever after influencing all downstream flow, but that it was instead simply the river itself: more water flowing, always flowing.

My point being, that none of it can be controlled.

And again, perhaps it is this simple: how powerful, natural, and necessary it is to our imaginations that that wild and rare bird had a place to fly off to. It just vanished from sight and hearing when it went off deeper into the woods. And yet it didn't vanish. It—and our imagination with it—kept going, drawn on farther and further and gracefully, into the wilds.

MAYBE THIS IS WHAT I'M getting at, working my way toward in much the manner of Lowry trying to parse out those tracks, making wider and wider circles—glimpsing the one path, then losing it; picking it up again, only to have it vanish into the brush again.

Wilderness is not necessary to develop a love of nature in children. I'm convinced we're born with a reverence for the natural and original world, and that that affinity can then only be strengthened, maintained, corroded, or buried—like anything else in the world.

The joy, the illumination, the realization or remembrance of that love can be stimulated by one ant, one sparrow, one seashell held to one's ear. In this regard, the pastoral can be, and often is, every bit as powerful as the wilderness. But wilderness is still the long-ago mother of the pastoral, the roots of the pastoral, and occupies a critical place in our imagination, which, or so the scientists tell us, is one of the things that most defines us as humans.

Without wilderness, we compromise our ability to imagine further.

Without wilderness, we become less human. Whether we like it or hate it or are indifferent to it is beside the point: we need it.

Surely there will always be ants, geraniums, deer tracks, and bird-calls for children to ponder over and be smitten and captivated by.

But they should have the choice—should retain the choice—of being able to decide whether to travel even farther and further then, with that love, and that imagining, if they so desire.

We should all have that choice. It is, and should remain, one of the tenets of our culture, and one of the spiritual as well as physical riches of a great and powerful civilization.

BACK AT THE RANCH, the wild Montana girls are sitting in lawn chairs, out in the cow pasture, feet propped up, wearing their sunglasses and swimsuits, beach towels over their shoulder, books in hand. The only sight more surreal than the scraggly bonsai reach of the thorny limbs of the weesatche and gnarled mesquite trees around them are the endless anthill-like mounds of manure, the scattered horse pods and cow pies.

But there's space, a comfortable amount of space, and there's also the exquisite luxury, to our Pacific Northwest psyches, of sunlight in the winter. A physical model, perhaps—that yellow light pouring down upon us—for how it is in our interiors, in those unmappable but deeply recognizable moments when that larger grace, and the hint of a larger understanding, or at least a larger acknowledging, pours down upon us.

Will these vacation days spent in another, more pastoral landscape, become some of the illuminating moments—and if so, how might that affect who these girls become? Or will these soft vacation days more likely be folded into the braid, the daily and nightly river, mixing in with mountain lion and bull elk, and simply continuing on, helping to form the horizontal platform or foundation, rather than any highly visible vertical structure?

Again, only after we have travelled farther downriver will any of us be able to pause in an eddy and look back and decide, and remember. But once more, the present seems clear: we need as many natural places—as wide and diverse a mix as is possible—the wild and the pastoral both, and the swamps and mountains and forests, and all the different types of forests, and all the different types of deserts and coastlines and grasslands as we can possibly retain. Whatever the wild or natural world has, it is part of us, part of who we are, and always have been, as well as who we are becoming. As we lose those landscapes, these experiences, one by one, our imaginations and even our spirits may become as barren as a wash or gully in a dry land through which water once murmured, and alongside which cool shade trees grew, but no more.

You don't have to go down to that river—you don't even have to like such rivers—but we must retain them, all the different kinds of nature, and we must afford the most immediate and secure protection to the rarest kinds—the fast-vanishing wilderness.

I have been speaking of children, but now I understand that I am speaking to and of myself, and of the person I have become, and of the child I was; of one of the various paths that have opened before me, and which I had the freedom to choose.

TRADITION CAN BE A LANDSCAPE—can be like a wilderness secure forever, unerodable—and story, or memory, can be another of the physical senses, a kind of seventh sense, as deeply felt as any touch or odour or taste or sight, as deeply felt as any intuition or song.

Imagine, then, please, the sweetness I encounter on those occasions when I am able to bring my Montana girls out of the wilderness and down to the same pastoral landscapes I inhabited at their age—the pastoral farm, with its muddy stock tanks to fish, rather than high, pristine mountain lakes; and then, later in this vacation, to the deer pasture itself, the one-time ultimate arbiter of wildness to a young boy, but a quantum step down, in wildness, to these girls . . .

Imagine the wonderful disorientation I feel as we arrive there at night, with jackrabbits bounding in front of the beam of our headlights, zigging and zagging in all directions as Mary Katherine gets out to open the gate.

The same scents, the same sounds, and even the same stories, there at the camp house that night. We build a bonfire of cedar in the same firepit and sit outside looking up at the same stars, and despite the fact that the lions and bears and wolves and jaguars are gone, it is still its own kind of wildness, to me, if not to these girls—though

I can also say truthfully that if the farther horizons of Montana's wildernesses no longer existed, this place, too, and even its stories and traditions, would lose some of its wildness, wildness finally seeping out of this place, and all the other ones like it, in the manner of blood trickling from a wound that will not heal . . .

There is no wound here yet. The remaining Montana wilderness, though not yet protected—over six million acres hanging in the balance year after year, debated by Congress—is still alive. The deer pasture itself—rocks and cactus and hardscrabble cedar—is still its own place, an island in a dramatically changing world.

The sameness of these things allows us—encourages us—to change: to grow and reach and stretch, to dive deep and travel far. To return, dream, and imagine. To go away and to return—becoming as shaped, in our travels, as any of the other enduring shapes in the world: the mountain that looks like the profile of a sleeping woman, the tree that looks like the silhouette of an old man with his arms outstretched.

The child standing next to a creek in the fog with a flashlight, peering down at a school of translucent, suspended fish is little different, thirty years later, from the young girls stalking along that same creek, trying to sneak up on, with their own flashlights, the night frogs and crawdads.

A clamant wildness, irrepressible, running beneath the surfaces, and across the surface, and just above the surface. A clamant wildness in the heart of the farthest roadless area, a clamant wildness in the sight of a single butterfly, in a suburban backyard. A clamant wildness in a single story, told or dreamed or remembered, and a clamant wildness in the touch of a single rough stone, gripped in the palm of one's hand.

We need it all. We do not have to go looking for any farther or further wildness, but we need to know, or at least be able to imagine, that it exists. We need to be able to at least hear the echo of where we came from, even if a long time ago, and barely or dimly remembered now.

We need the dream of such a past, and the promise or at least the opportunity of such a future.

The green pastoral meadows sculpt us, the city parks and gardens sculpt us, and even now, the last few blank spots on the map sculpt us. They are all but shades of one continuum, and we need them all, and our children deserve the possibility of it all. They demand it, and we must—must—deliver it.

MARGARET ATWOOD

Cryogenics A SYMPOSIUM

MARGARET ATWOOD *is the author of more than twenty-five books of poetry, fiction, and nonfiction. Her work has been translated into more than thirty languages and has won numerous awards. She is the author of the novels* Surfacing, The Handmaid's Tale, *and* Alias Grace, *among others, as well as* The Blind Assassin, *winner of the 2000 Booker Prize. She lives in Toronto.*

A: When I'm sixty-five I'm going to get my head cut off and flash-frozen. They've already got the technology, they've set up the corporations ... Then it'll stay frozen until they've learned how to clone the rest of my body from a single cell, and they'll thaw out my head and reattach it. By that time, I figure the environment and all that stuff will be through the downturn and things will be more straightened out.

B: I take it you think your mind will survive the process, memories intact?

A: That would be the idea.

C: Mind, or brain? Some people think the two are not coextensive. For instance, your brain might be a sort of grey Tastee-Freez, while your mind ...

B: How about freezer burn? Ever seen frozen eyes? They go the colour of ...

C: Would your new body be sixty-five too?

D: This Chilean sea bass is yummy!

B: We shouldn't be eating it. They're wiping it out. They are actually strip-mining the entire ocean. They're aiming for a huge underwater golf course.

D: I know, I know, but I forgot, and anyway it's already cooked.

A: I was thinking more like twenty-three for the body.

C: So you're going to have this wrinkly old head on top of a beef-cake? Not very delectable.

D: I wouldn't want to climb in the sack with something like that!

A: You won't be around, honey-bunny. Anyway, they'll do plastic surgery. I'll look great. But I'll get to keep the wisdom I'll have accumulated by then.

E: You are a dreamer! The whole thing is *so* grotesque!

A: New scientific ideas always seem grotesque to the masses.

E: I am *not* the masses! Anyway, what would stop them from taking your money—then, after a few years with your head in the freezer, they'd declare bankruptcy and pull out the plug and toss your head in the garbage? That's what they'll do!

A: No need to be rude. I have faith in the process.

C: I've got a worse idea! They unfreeze your head and hook it up to a monitor and run your most painful memories on it as cheap entertainment. Your whole life would be a sideshow freak!

K: Or there would be a natural catastrophe—an earthquake, a tornado—the grid goes down—your head rots . . . Could you pass the slave-worker poison-sprayed artificially ripened grapes please, and yes, I know I shouldn't have bought them. I did wash them, though. So don't worry.

A: I've thought of that. They'll have solar panels, with the lines running down into a shockproof underground cavern . . .

B: Look, let's face it. Pollution, vanishing ozone layer, genetically engineered organisms go on the rampage, the icebergs melt, the sea floods all coastal plains, plagues wipe out civilization . . . Only a few survive, reduced to roaming bands of brutal scavengers. They travel at night to avoid the deadly rays of the sun, and, all large land mammals having gone extinct, they eat rats, cockroaches, roots, and one another.

A: I'll be sleeping out that part, remember?

B: Wait . . . they come upon the underground cavern. There's no guards anymore and the hinges have rusted off the door. The nomads break in, they pry open the fridge, and what do they see?

D: A wedge of leftover Brie, half a head of celery, a thing of yogurt *way* past the sell-by date . . . Let's have coffee. This is shade-grown coffee, so don't look at me like that. Oh yeah, they also find that damn pike you caught last summer, sweetie. It's stinking up the entire freezer—what exactly are your plans for it?

B: Don't be frivolous. This is about his head. They open the freezer, and they see . . .

C: I think I know where this is going.

B: They see protein! They say, Get the cooking pot. They say, Feast time!

A: You are a pathetic, sick, psychically damaged individual.

B: I'm just a realist.

C: Same thing.

DAVID REYNOLDS

Taking a Shower with
William Hazlitt

DAVID REYNOLDS *was one of the founders of Bloomsbury*
Publishing, where he was Deputy Managing Director
and Publishing Director (nonfiction) until 1999,
when he left to concentrate on writing. He is the
author of the acclaimed memoir Swan River.
He lives in London, England.

I WAS WALKING FAST UPHILL. It was late in February, cold, the sky a pale grey, the sun a silvery haze, low in the southwest behind the sycamores, weak enough to look at. There weren't many people around: just Reuben, Chrissy, one-legged Ellen, and the young, thin-faced girl whose name I didn't know; and somewhere among us there were two or three others, just nodding acquaintances or less. We were ahead of the evening rush, had the whole glorious, open space to ourselves: we people who don't have regular jobs.

Chrissy, the bleached-blonde, self-styled leader of the pack, who leads with her chin and her arms and her elbows, was striding confidently as usual. If I met her eyes, she would speak to me; even gasping for breath, with the sweat streaming, she would always find the energy to talk—usually about something inconsequential. I went on walking, eyes to the front, calf muscles screaming.

Reuben, my mentor, big and black and always reassuring, was off to my right taking a rest, sitting down knees up, head in hands, as if it had been a long day. Elegant Ellen was lying on her front, crutches to one side, pulling on her lone ankle, stretching her thigh muscle. Perhaps she had a cramp, but I knew she wouldn't accept help in any circumstances.

The thin-faced girl was tiring, but determined, pushing herself on and up, hands on knees, straggly dark hair wagging from side to side. She would get there; she always did, but I had worried about her for a few weeks now, since the day I heard her tell someone about herself—someone she knew but hadn't seen for a while, it seemed. I shouldn't have listened, but I couldn't help it; we were walking close to one another at the same speed. It hadn't been good: parents had had money trouble, moved far away; drugs and something faintly criminal had led her to some kind of enforced rehabilitation, from which she was now allowed out to join us here.

I thought about what Jonathan had said in the pub the night before. "You're going to a *gym*? Walking fast uphill, cycling, rowing? Why the hell don't you just walk fast across the common, get a bike, join a rowing club?" He had sucked on his pint and looked away in disgust.

He was right in a way, but this was more practical, I had told him, and I liked it: the routine; the sleek, grey machines with their winking lights and their yellow, illuminated numerals, which told me times, distances, calories expended, anything I could conceivably want to know, if I pushed the right button enough times. There were Reuben and the other instructors to encourage me, to tell me what to do, given my age, height, weight, fat percentage, and general level of fitness. And there was the camaraderie with people I barely knew—ordinary people, natural people. An inexpensive local gym— no athletes, film stars, supermodels, princesses—just people who live or work around here, people of every fat percentage.

I went on thinking as I slurped up water at the communal spout in the corner and began my twelve minutes of cycling—on the interval program, with the computer set to resistance levels 2 and 4. Just to say that the gym was practical and I liked it wasn't good enough, because the same things could be said of a fast walk on the common. I like the common, and it's immensely practical; it's even nearer my house than the gym. So why wasn't I out there, breathing fresh air, listening to the birds, looking at the trees and the flowers, feeling the warmth of the sun or the damp of the rain? I like these things; I always have. Why, then, do I want to be in this air-conditioned, concrete barn with just one window overlooking a clump of scrawny sycamores, five television channels projected onto the white wall in front of me, and the incessant bass thud of music that I would normally walk a long way fast, even uphill, to avoid?

I pedalled vigorously, and vigorously tried to think. There had to be something about working out in the gym—beyond the routine, beyond the machines governed by computers, the presence of helpful instructors, and the elusive, almost imaginary connection with a few people I barely knew—something fundamental, to do with my nature, perhaps with human nature—and not so much *beyond* those things, but *beneath* them: something deep down.

It's good to think in a gym. The ability to ease your mind away from what you are doing and skive off somewhere else is almost essential; otherwise twelve minutes on a stationary bike can become never-ending, unendurable, almost Sisyphean. But on this occasion my twelve minutes passed slowly; there were longueurs when my mind drifted from the search for the profundities of the gymnasium to the banal projected images of a television quiz show and a pop music video. When the longed-for message "Course complete. Prepare for cool-down" finally appeared, my brain had moved no further than my body.

As I crossed the floor to the rowing machine, I decided to come at the conundrum from another angle: why do I like nature? And my brain went into overdrive. Why, to me, is a landscape devoid of any mark of humanity preferable to this state-of-the-art gymnasium or, for that matter, to the streets, bars, restaurants, jazz clubs of Soho, a district of London that I know well and also love, or to any of the great monuments to man's inventiveness, industry, and aesthetic sensibility: the Parthenon, the Taj Mahal, the Alhambra, the Empire State Building, all of which I have gazed at and appreciated? Why, to reduce the matter to its essentials, is a single flower—say, a primrose—preferable to the pyramids or to the ceiling of the Sistine Chapel?

Or *is it?* I heaved yet more heavily on my artificial oar. I love those things too, don't I? They are beautiful, awe-inspiring, a testimony to the worth of the human race. Do I really think a single flower is better than these things? Does anyone think that? What about Wordsworth?

> *To me the meanest flower that blows can give*
> *Thoughts that do often lie too deep for tears.*
> ("Intimations of Immortality from Recollections of Early Childhood")

But then, he also wrote, of the view from Westminster Bridge at the heart of London, then the biggest city in the world:

> *Earth has not anything to show more fair:*
> *Dull would he be of soul who could pass by*
> *A sight so touching in its majesty:*
> *This City now doth, like a garment, wear*
> *The beauty of the morning; silent, bare . . .*
> ("Composed Upon Westminster Bridge Sept. 3, 1802")

SURELY THERE IS NO NEED to compare nature with, rank it against, the finest achievements of man. Isn't this as fatuous a procedure as the popular journalist's pastime of compiling lists of the best-ever pop songs, movies, women's legs, or moments in sport? One cannot sensibly or usefully produce a top ten of the world's most beautiful buildings—who is to say that the cathedral at Chartres is better than the Ibn Tulun mosque? And to bring nature into competition with these things is all the more absurd, as it would be to compare one facet of nature with another. Which is better? The Victoria Falls, the Grand Canyon, or the Himalayas?

So a primrose is *not*, after all, better than Michelangelo's *David* or Mozart's Clarinet Concerto. It is different. Nature is different.

My ten minutes on the rowing machine had hardly happened at all. My biceps and triceps were aching and bulging—proof that I *had* been simulating rowing, that my bottom *had* been sliding purposefully to and fro on a plastic seat along a chromium rod—but my brain seemed to have travelled in a circle. The thin-faced girl had her back to me, small grey patches of sweat discernible on her off-white T-shirt; she was still entrapped on the cross-trainer, a hateful device seemingly designed to simulate walking uphill while up to one's thighs in porridge.

Why *do* we do this?

I delivered a smile and a nod as I walked quickly past Chrissy and received a smirk and a flap of her elbows in response. A raised-eyebrow-and-"see ya" goodbye to Reuben, and I was soon showering and thinking about Hazlitt: William Hazlitt (1778–1830), English essayist, greatly admired in his own time and somewhat later by my father, whose books I inherited, among them a volume of Hazlitt's *Selected Essays*, published in 1941. In the thirty-three years since my father's death, I had lugged his library around, built shelves for it in a variety of flats and houses, and dipped into the comfortable, cloth-bound volume of Hazlitt fewer times than I would like.

I continued to think about Hazlitt as I peered into people's front gardens on my walk home: snowdrops nodding and crocuses preaching; daffodils, straight-backed, looking on. I was searching for primroses; someone had their close relative, the more highly bred purple primula, in a window box, but there was no hint of that dreamy washed-out yellow. Perhaps it was too early for them, or perhaps they are too wild, too uncultivated, for London gardeners. I had a faint memory that in one of his essays Hazlitt writes something profound about man's relationship with nature—something that had touched me when I read it years before—and that he mentions primroses. Hazlitt loved nature and the English countryside. He had a home in a village in Wiltshire, but he also had a house on Soho's Frith Street, now a hotel and close to the great Ronnie Scott's Jazz Club; he had loved country *and* town.

At home I found his essay "On the Love of the Country," first published in 1814. He begins by asserting that we do not love nature simply because it is "beautiful and magnificent." Rather, "it is because natural objects have been associated with the sports of our childhood, with air and exercise, with our feelings in solitude . . . with change of place, the pursuit of new scenes, and thoughts of distant friends; it is because they have surrounded us in almost all situations, in joy and in sorrow, in pleasure and in pain; because they have been one chief source and nourishment of our feelings, and a part of our being, that we love them as we do ourselves."

Well put—though not, perhaps, to us in the twenty-first century, an especially original notion. But Hazlitt then introduces another idea: the "transferable" aspect of our attachment to the objects of nature "which distinguishes this attachment from others . . . If I have once associated strong feelings of delight with the objects of natural scenery, the tie becomes indissoluble, and I shall ever after feel the same attachment to other objects of the same sort." Our relationships with humans, in contrast, are not transferable: "My having been attached to any particular person does not make me feel the same attachment to the next person I may chance to meet . . . But it is otherwise with respect to Nature. There is neither hypocrisy, caprice, nor mental reservation in her favours. Our intercourse with her is not liable to accident or change, interruption or disappointment. She smiles on us still the same."

I had gone to Hazlitt hoping for an insight into my love of nature that might lead me on to an understanding of why I preferred to exercise at the gym. And I may have found it, but I was also searching him for primroses. And I found them, embedded in an example he gives to support his thesis that it is the associations we make with nature, rather than its intrinsic beauty, that thrill us: "I love to see the trees first covered with leaves in the spring, the primroses peeping out from some sheltered bank and the innocent lambs running races on the soft green turf; because, at that birth-time of Nature, I have always felt sweet hopes and happy wishes—which have not been fulfilled!"

One of my earliest memories is of primroses. I am walking with my father uphill along a lane. We are on our way to a wood to fill a sack with something I have not heard of before, leaf mould, for the garden. I am four, or perhaps five. There is a steep, grass-covered bank, overhung by a dark hedge; thick roots, coated with moss and tangled with ivy, protrude here and there. The grass is the new green of spring, and sprinkled across it are the whites, yellows, pinks, blues, and purples of small flowers. Everything is a little damp—I can smell it—although the sun is filtering through bare trees on the other side of the lane.

I feel a sense of wonder, of revelation—a feeling like the one I get when I am given a new and exciting toy—and I am attracted to a patch of pale yellow flowers, circled by soft, oval leaves, low to the ground. They are a little larger than the rest, open and inviting. I look at the symmetrical arrangement of petals and see a thin orange ring close to the heart of each flower. I lean forward and sniff and find a new, delicate scent.

My father says the name, "primroses," and suggests I pick a few to give to my mother as a present. "But only pick one from each clump," he says, "and pick low down so that there is a long stalk." I do as I am told and make the long walk home, clutching six or seven stalks that grow ever more limp in the warmth of my hand. My mother seems delighted. She hugs me and carefully arranges the expiring primroses in a small glass, and I have a sense that something is not quite right, that the primroses are dying and should still be in the lane. I sniff them again and the scent is still there, a scent I will always remember—for me, the essence of spring.

I am sure then that Hazlitt is right, that the associations we make with nature come from childhood—provided, of course, that we are lucky enough to encounter nature when we are young. I was lucky. I lived in a house with a small garden, where my parents grew flowers and vegetables, in a small town, from which, when I was a little older, I could walk with my friends into the countryside and, in particular, to a wood on the bank of the river where there was a painted sign: Bird Sanctuary—Keep Out—Trespassers Will Be

Prosecuted. To a small group of ten-year-old boys, this was, of course, an invitation that led to a habit of climbing the fence when there was no one about, creeping through dank undergrowth, climbing huge trees, straddling a branch, and looking down at the swans on the river, the cows in the neighbouring fields, and the mass of dead leaves on the ground below.

We played football, and cops and robbers, and shouted and fought with each other somewhere else. But there, in the forbidden wood, we were in thrall to a force that we couldn't have defined, a force that dispensed stillness and the kind of idle contemplation that prompts the picking up of a stick and the pushing of it into the ground, for no reason except to see and smell and feel the earth.

My father's job was another piece of my early luck. He was a seed salesman and spent his days driving from farm to farm, persuading their owners to buy his employer's range of seeds—principally wheat, barley, oats, and kale, which they grew to feed to their cattle. He covered a large area, from the Thames Valley up into the Chiltern Hills, and I often went with him, map reading, helping to find remote farms that he hadn't visited before, and rolling his eternal cigarettes. He knew his business, and his customers often sought his advice, which meant that I spent time in fields and farmyards half-listening to arcane discussions about such things as "yields," "straight ears," and "one-year leys." Sometimes a farmer would want his opinion of the soil in a particular field, and we would tramp a mile or more over the hills in our Wellingtons; my father would pick up a handful of earth, poke at it with his finger, and discourse on drainage, wind, rain, and the movement of the sun.

I got to know and love much of the landscape of that part of England and soon realized that though it had changed little in centuries, most of it was manmade, created by the felling of ancient forests, the ploughing of soil, and the planting of hedges. It was, and is, nature tamed, but I came across it as a child and so any small sign of it, like the "little spot of green" that Rousseau could see from his window in Annecy, will do.

BEYOND THE SOLITARY WINDOW, sunlight falls on the branches of the sycamores, creating an action painting in light and shade; buds are forming and the sharp lines of winter are beginning to waver. In a month or so, this window too will have its little spot of green. I have smiled at my acquaintances and stretched my quads and abductors in the manner laid down by Reuben, so I am fast-walking uphill again and thinking fast as well, phrasing in my mind what I shall say to Jonathan when I see him tomorrow, because thanks to Hazlitt I have a satisfactory, and to me satisfying, answer.

The common close to my home is some forty miles from the farms in the Chilterns and the lane where the primroses grew in the 1950s. But the associations are numerous and transferable. Although it is only five miles from Hyde Park Corner—by some standards the centre of London—the common is wilder than farmland because "common land," which was so designated in most parts of England in the Middle Ages, was not for cultivation but primarily for the grazing of farm animals. Since 1871 this particular common has been protected by Act of Parliament, and soon afterwards the few locals who still had grazing rights—the last was a Mrs. Morrison, who kept geese—lost their rights and were paid compensation. The land is managed by locally elected "conservators," no building is permitted, and although there is a cricket pitch and some open grassland, which is mown once or twice a year, much of it is wild or, at least, what North Americans call "protected wilderness."

I walk there often, watching the seasons change, the birds court and nest, the skies changing formations and colours. I especially like to lean on a narrow footbridge above the overgrown brook that flows down to the Thames and see ducks and moorhens and water rats and occasionally the shadowy outline of a fish. Once, I caught the dazzling blue of a kingfisher, still for a moment and then flashing over the water. I walk there, but I don't walk fast. I go to the gym for that: for aerobic exercise, what Reuben calls "the cardiovascular," and for the stretches he has prescribed for me; it is warm, or cool, depending on the weather outside, and there are thick, rubber mats. As I said to the cynical Jonathan, "I like it and it's practical."

But Hazlitt has shown me the deeper reason. The pleasure I derive from nature will always have associations with childhood, but my decision to exercise is very much a product of middle age; it's something I didn't contemplate until I passed fifty and saw that my joyful and inspirational amblings on the common were not enough to compensate my body for the hours it spends folded up, fixed to a chair, while only my fingers move, to prod a keyboard and slide a mouse. And then Reuben explained about the cardiovascular and the need to stretch my muscles until they ache.

So this is good for me, this stationary computerized bicycling— and, no doubt, for Chrissy and Ellen and the thin-faced girl—*and* it makes me feel better. But the farmers my father and I used to visit were happily unaware of their fat percentage and their metabolic rate, because such measures have no connection with nature, which kept them healthy and which nurtures me in another way, by connecting me to the spirit in every living thing. Awareness of the empirical detail of one's own body belongs in another place. To walk fast uphill across the common would be to miss, or worse, ignore, the point. This is what I shall tell Jonathan.

And I'll tell him to take a shower and think of Hazlitt. I'll keep to myself the word *synergy*, a term now besmirched by the panjandrums of industry as an excuse for snapping up someone else's enterprise; Jonathan is sensitive underneath, and he would struggle to disentangle my meaning from his suspicions of large-scale business. But for me, though the two run in parallel and, but for the sycamores, do not meet, there is a synergy between my love of the common and my use of the gym. If I were a farmer or an outdoor manual worker or a hunter-gatherer, nature would supply both my spiritual and my physical needs, but as it is, I am right to take advantage of what civilization and urbanization have to offer. The Greeks and Romans had gymnasia, after all; the root of the word is the Greek *gumnos*, meaning "bare" or "naked," and the first gyms were places where young men exercised naked—perhaps in an attempt to return to a state of nature.

Maybe I *will* tell him about synergy and the Greeks, and there's something else I could tell him as well, because I'm remembering now that there is another side to my early relationship with nature— and perhaps, therefore, to my curious attachment to this gym. But Hazlitt probably can't help me with this, because as far as I am aware, he never trod on a palm-fringed beach or travelled in Africa.

As a child, in the years when I was gaining a love of the tamed nature of the English home counties, I was also being seduced by jungles, mountains, remote rivers, and, more than any of those, desert islands: places where no humans, or very few, had ever been—

untamed nature. It began when my father bought me an edition of Daniel Defoe's *Robinson Crusoe*—abridged for children, but there was still plenty to read. I was six or seven and absorbed it avidly, lying for hours on my bed, studying the lifelike black line drawings of a man dressed in animal skins, alone among palm trees; of the single footprint in the sand; of the hesitant emergence from the forest of Man Friday. I was enthralled and for years after wanted to be alone, but not for too long, on a desert island. Learning from my father that the story was based on real events that happened to a real sailor called Alexander Selkirk intensified my sense of awe and excitement; such things really happened.

The feeling was different from the sense of wonder induced by the primroses and the country lane in spring. The book made me want to do something one day, perhaps to escape, for a while at least, from the world I knew; but there was an association in my mind with the natural world—because Crusoe was alone, until Friday's appearance, in nature.

After *Robinson Crusoe*, my father provided in quick succession *The Swiss Family Robinson*; R. M. Ballantyne's *Coral Island*, the story on which William Golding based *Lord of the Flies*; and Robert Louis Stevenson's *Treasure Island*—all desert-island stories and all entrancing to a small boy growing up in a small town in northern Europe.

My obsession deepened over the next year or two, as I read about other exotic, faraway places, where man had had no influence and where experiencing nature was an obligatory adventure instead of a voluntary stroll. I read two anthologies, *Great True Adventures in Ice and Snow* and *Great Stories of the Wild West*; biographies of David Livingstone and Cecil Rhodes—in their different ways, explorers and founders of colonial Africa; Edgar Wallace's popular novel set in

Kenya, *Sanders of the River*; and a book called *Three Singles to Adventure*—Adventure is the name of a town in what is now Guyana—by a young zoologist named Gerald Durrell.

Of course, this was a love affair of the head, conducted while I lay on my bed reading, and it remained unfulfilled. Then I went to a new school and had less time for reading of my own choice, and on through university to the world of jobs—and somewhere along the way the passion faded and I forgot about empty landscapes and deserted beaches curving around warm seas.

I was reminded of them in 1974, when there was famine in Ethiopia. Few in the West knew about it—it would be eleven years before Bob Geldof and a group of rock stars would sing about another famine in that beautiful country. I knew about it, though, and sought out the few, brief reports consigned to the middle pages of the newspapers, because I had a friend who was working for UNICEF in Addis Ababa. I didn't know exactly what she was doing, only that emaciated people, wrapped in dust-coloured cloths and carrying babies, were tramping tens, sometimes hundreds, of miles in a search for food; that thousands were dying; and that my friend was somehow helping. I was twenty-five, living comfortably in London and for the first time earning money by writing—an achievement that gave me some satisfaction, though the job, writing a guidebook for *Reader's Digest*, was hardly glamorous. Eventually I grew tired of it—and my friend wrote from Addis Ababa suggesting I go there for a holiday.

A holiday in a country riven by famine? Surely not. It was inappropriate. If I were to go there, I should work, do something useful. But, no, she wrote back, the agencies didn't need anyone—especially not someone with no useful training. I should just come, stay a few weeks, travel the country, and, if I had time, move on to somewhere else, perhaps Kenya to the south, where my friend had other friends. In short, I should have a holiday in Africa.

The suggestion was enticing, exciting, but a little scary; I had never left Europe or been anywhere wilder than the lochs of Scotland and the olive groves of Corfu. Another letter came. One of my friend's friends, an American Peace Corps volunteer based in Kenya, knew some priests who owned a house, for use as a retreat, close to a remote village, fifty miles north of Mombasa. The priests were rarely there, and they allowed the Peace Corps man to use their house when he wanted a break from his work. I could stay in this house if I wished. It was isolated, set among palm trees, facing a beach on the edge of the Indian Ocean.

I flew on January 16, 1975. Within two days, I was in the passenger seat of a Land Rover at the head of a convoy of Land Rovers ready to drive north out of Addis Ababa—beside me a tall, narrow-boned Amhara called Derbi; beyond him, in the driver's seat, Elroy, a Canadian veterinarian, wearing a cowboy hat. For the next three days, whenever the convoy was ready to move, Elroy took hold of his hat, pushed it through the window, waved it in a forward direction, and shouted, "Move 'em out." I spent five days with Elroy, Derbi, and ten others. We travelled four hundred miles and reached the hot, dusty town of Lalibela, famous for its churches carved out of red rock. There Elroy and his veterinary team camped and began a lengthy program of vaccinating cattle. I moved on, northwest by bus to the ancient city of Gondar and then south again to Addis.

I spent six weeks in this way, taking trips in every direction from Addis Ababa with new friends who worked for aid agencies. I watched them and the people and the landscape, and, if I was feeling analytical,

I thought about politics and economics and a little about agriculture—many of my kind chauffeurs were involved in projects connected with farming. I simply admired—and sometimes gawped, slack-jawed, at—the sights outside the shabby, smelly city: vast golden plains; flat-topped mountain ridges, piled up one behind another, receding into the heat; flocks of flamingos standing up to their backward-pointing knees in perfectly circular crater lakes; proud, glistening Galla women and their deep-black, bare-chested men; empty deserts to the east and the south; and close to the capital, quiet, biblical hills with self-explanatory names, Toothbrush and Crewcut. But beyond cursing the scant rainfall, which had brought about drought and famine, I didn't *think* about nature. It was just there, often barren, but beautiful amid the politics, poverty, and disease.

In Kenya and Tanzania, where rain and crops and wildlife were more abundant, and where children died from lack of medical care rather than starvation, I felt similarly. I didn't think about Mount Kilimanjaro, the Serengeti Plain, or the Ngorongoro Crater, with its zebra, rhinoceros, lions, and vultures; I experienced them, admired them simply because they existed, naturally. And then, for the last week of my journey, I came to the house among the palms on the edge of the ocean, four degrees south of the Equator.

Remembering the place, I can feel the dry, burning heat and see the yellow light on the soft mulch beneath the trees, the cool, grey shadows on the brown earth, the blue-green of the ocean, and the flat whiteness of the beach, flecked by shards of seaweed, brittle and blackened by the sun. I spent seven days there, shifting between the house, the sea, and the village—a mile away, beyond the palm and mango wood, where I bought bread, tinned mackerel, and Coca-Cola.

It didn't match my boyhood dream, and I saw, even then, that it was foolish to have thought that it might. The palms in the wood were the stuff of dreams, tall, silver-barked, slender, and gracefully curving, but those by the beach were stunted, their trunks angled, crowns lopsided, fronds tangled, in an effort, it seemed, to flee the sea and salt. The colours—greens, browns, blues, and greys—were cast in a harsh, unfamiliar, ochrous-white light, the only punctuation the occasional, papery cerise of bougainvillea. The air was dry and, like the sand on the beach, too hot for a man from a temperate world, fifty-five degrees of latitude to the north. Through the bulk of the day I stayed indoors or in shade, reading or writing in my notebook.

At first the diet of tinned mackerel and the frequent visits of curious villagers irritated me. Perhaps they didn't fit with my residual juvenile vision of a solitary existence where I sustained myself by catching fish and climbing trees for coconuts. But then I saw that Robinson Crusoe, the Swiss family Robinson, and the boys who were cast away on Ballantyne's coral island didn't *want* to be there, were *not* enjoying an idyll, were just surviving, doing the best they could while longing for escape. And I realized that despite being marooned for only a week—and marooned only in my imagination and by my own pride, for a long walk and a bus ride would take me back to Mombasa—I was feeling as they did and that the friendly people and the one shop with its scanty supplies of food were an aid at least— and perhaps essential—to my surviving this self-imposed exile.

INSTEAD OF THE DAYTIME HANDFUL, there is a herd. I have come in late. Reuben is off duty, replaced by Neil and his hair gel; Chrissy, Ellen, and the thin-faced girl have gone, and in their place, there's a sound like stampeding cattle as twenty-five office workers pound the line of treadmills in pace with the mechanical beat of garage music. I wait my turn, climb on, and force myself to escape to that week, all those years ago, on the coast of East Africa. And I see that my problem was simple. I was away from home ground, in an unfamiliar natural environment, and for the first time in my life I was out of touch with Europeans, North Americans, Australians, all of the kinds of people with whom unconsciously, habitually, daily, I had been sharing experiences, not just since my arrival in Africa, but since I was born. In that sense, though it was less dramatic than it sounds, I was more alone than I had ever been.

Later, as I shower, I think again of Hazlitt. Somehow I now associate him with the warm, taut, deep-lunged feeling that comes over me after a workout, and therefore with the hot rain of the shower and the plastic soap bottle with its nifty integral hook. Hazlitt's theory of the transferability of our attachment from one natural object to another is correct but needs qualification, it seems to me. The attachment is transferable, but it weakens in proportion to the distance we travel from the natural surroundings of our childhood toward the Equator or the pole. Below the Equator, for those who grow up north of it, the attachment probably strengthens as they journey farther south; the New Zealand countryside, for example, is sometimes said to be like England's.

There is a hint in Hazlitt's "On the Love of the Country" that he understood this. Of a visit to Paris, he writes: "I remember when I was abroad, the trees, and grass and wet leaves, rustling in the walks of the Tuileries, seemed to be as much English, to be as much the same trees and grass, that I had always been used to, as the sun shining over my head was the same sun which I saw in England." The fact that he remarks on this suggests that he expected otherwise, and had he travelled farther south—to the shore of the Indian Ocean, north of Mombasa, for example—my guess is that he would have found otherwise, felt more as I did.

Walking home, past the tidy front gardens where many of the daffodils, victims of a late-February gale, now kiss the ground, I recall an essay by the American writer and traveller Barry Lopez. It is called "The American Geographies"* and it is a fine and, to my mind, important plea for the preservation of accurate and authentic local knowledge and for people to pay attention to the geography of their own natural place—which, in the twenty-first century, as Lopez points out, may well be urban rather than rural.

Lopez argues that our knowledge of small-scale environments, of a size that people might call home—a small town, a river basin, a few blocks of New York City—is now threatened by artificial national geographies, homogenized, idealized visions of nature that treat huge tracts of land as if they were a single entity. These false geographies—Lopez writes about the United States, but his observations apply almost everywhere—are foisted on us by politics, business, advertising, and movies, forces whose interests are served by manipulating and standardizing our attitudes to our environment. These inaccurate, often glamorized and idealized, interpretations of the natural world are increasingly widely accepted, because so many people are ignorant of geography in general and of the natural history of their own localities in particular. The dangers are that this unwitting acceptance of falsehood lays us open to political and commercial manipulation and, more importantly, cuts us off from the truths of our world and of our existence.

* Reprinted in Barry Lopez, *About This Life: Journeys on the Threshold of Memory* (New York: Alfred A. Knopf, 1998; London: The Harvill Press, 1999).

I wonder whether Hazlitt's theory and my qualification of it—that we are attached to nature by our childhood experience, but less so the farther we travel from the site of that experience—doesn't chime, however faintly, with Lopez's alarm. Once or twice a year I return to the small town and the surrounding lanes and farmland where I grew up. I find it hard to explain why, but perhaps there is something instinctive that causes me to cleave to the landscape that aroused emotions in me as a child. Maybe I should nurture that instinct, accept that one locality means more to me than others, accept that when I travel I will find something different; that it is fruitless to seek similarities with what I know and far better to seek to understand what I don't know.

Which returns me to my gym, because gyms—like outlets of McDonald's—bear no relation to nature, are not different in London, Toronto, or Delhi. If I want to walk fast purely for exercise, I *should* go to a gym and leave the commons and the farms, the Tuileries and the tropical beaches, for locals and visitors who want to contemplate nature. And I shall tell Jonathan that as well.

WADE DAVIS

The Day the Waylakas Dance

WADE DAVIS *has a Ph.D. in ethnobotany from Harvard
University and is currently Explorer-in-Residence at the National
Geographic Society. He is the author of numerous books,
including the international bestseller* The Serpent and the
Rainbow, The Clouded Leopard, Light at the
Edge of the World, *and* One River, *a finalist for the
Governor General's Award. He lives with his wife and
two children in Washington, D.C., and spends the
summers in the Stikine wilderness of British Columbia.*

WHEN I FIRST TRAVELLED DOWN the spine of the Andean Cordillera, past the remnants of temples and enormous storehouses that once fed armies in their thousands, through valleys transformed by agricultural terraces, past narrow tracks of flat stones—all that remains of the fourteen thousand miles of roads that once bound the Inca Empire—it was difficult to imagine how so much could have been accomplished in less than a century. The empire, which stretched over three thousand miles, was the largest ever forged on the American continent. Within its boundaries lived nearly all the people of the Andean world. There was said to be no hunger. All matter was perceived as divine, Earth itself the womb of creation.

When the Spaniards saw the monuments of the Inca, they could not believe them to be the work of men. The Catholic Church declared the stonework to be the product of demons, an assertion no more fantastic than more recent speculation that the masonry was of extraterrestrial origin. There was, of course, no magic technique. Only time, immense levies of workers, and an attitude toward stone that most Westerners find impossible to comprehend.

In the early spring of 1975, I visited the sacred valley of the Urubamba for the first time. As I walked the ruins of Pisac, a redoubt perched on a high mountain spur, I saw that the entire face of the massif was transformed by terraces, which, when viewed from afar, took on the form of a gigantic condor, wings spread wide as if to protect the fortress. The river far below had been channelled by the Inca, lined for much of its length with stone walls to protect fields from flooding and to maximize agricultural production in one of the most fertile valleys of the empire. The faint remains of other terraces marked every mountainside. The entire landscape had been transformed, a stunning engineering feat for a people who knew nothing of the wheel and had no iron tools. As I sat in the Temple of the Moon, surrounded by some of the finest Inca masonry in existence, I recorded these notes in my journal and later incorporated them into the book *One River:*

> For the people of the Andes, matter is fluid. Bones are not death but life crystallized, and thus potent sources of energy, like a stone charged by lightning or a plant brought into being by the sun. Water is vapor, a miasma of disease and mystery, but in its purest state it is ice, the shape of snowfields on the flanks of mountains, the glaciers that are the highest and most sacred destination of the pilgrims. When an Inca mason placed his hands on rock, he did not feel cold granite; he sensed life, the power and resonance of the Earth within the stone. Transforming it into a perfect ashlar or a block of polygonal masonry was service to the Inca, and thus a gesture to the gods, and for such a task, time had no meaning. This attitude, once harnessed by an imperial system capable of recruiting workers by the thousand, made almost anything possible.
>
> If stones are dynamic, it is only because they are part of the

land, of Pachamama. For the people of the Andes, the Earth is
alive, and every wrinkle on the landscape, every hill and out-
crop, every mountain and stream has a name and is imbued
with ritual significance. The high peaks are addressed as Apu,
meaning "lord." Together the mountains are known as the
Tayakuna, the fathers, and some are so powerful that it can be
dangerous even to look at them. Other sacred places, a cave or
mountain pass, a waterfall where the rushing water speaks as
an oracle, are honored as the Tirakuna. These are not spirits
dwelling within landmarks. Rather, the reverence is for the
actual place itself.

A mountain is an ancestor, a protective being, and all those
living within the shadow of a high peak share in its benevolence or wrath. The rivers are the open veins of the Earth, the
Milky Way their heavenly counterpart. Rainbows are double-
headed serpents which emerge from hallowed springs, arch
across the sky, and bury themselves again in the earth.
Shooting stars are bolts of silver. Behind them lie all the heav-
ens, including the dark patches of cosmic dust, the negative
constellations which to the highland Indians are as meaningful
as the clusters of stars that form animals in the sky.

These notions of the sanctity of land were ancient in the Andes.
The Spanish did everything in their power to crush the spirit of the
people, destroying the temples, tearing asunder the sanctuaries, vio-
lating the offerings to the sun. But it was not a shrine that the
Indians worshipped, it was the land itself: the rivers and waterfalls,
the rocky outcrops and mountain peaks, the rainbows and stars.
Every time a Catholic priest planted a cross on top of an ancient site,

he merely confirmed in the eyes of the people the inherent sacredness of the place. In the wake of the Spanish Conquest, when the last of the temples lay in ruins, Earth endured, the one religious icon that even the Spaniards could not destroy. Through the centuries, the character of the relationship between the people and their land has changed, but not its fundamental importance.

ONE AFTERNOON LAST WINTER, in the small Andean town of Chinchero, just outside Cusco, I sat on a rock throne carved from granite. At my back was the sacred mountain Antakillqa, lost in dark clouds yet illuminated in a mysterious way by a rainbow that arched across its flank. Below, the terraces of Chinchero fell away to an emerald plain, the floor of an ancient seabed, beyond which rose the ridges of the distant Vilcabamba, the last redoubt of the Inca, a landscape of holy shrines and lost dreams where Tupac Amarú waged war and the spirit of the Sun still ruled for fifty years after the Conquest. Two young boys played soccer on the village green, a plaza where once Topa Inca Yupanqui, second of the great Inca rulers, reviewed his troops. On the very stone where I rested, he, no doubt, had stood, for this village of adobe and whitewashed homes, this warren of cobblestones, mud, and grass, had been built upon the ruins of his summer palace.

For four hundred years, the Catholic Church, perched at the height of the ruins overlooking the market square, had dominated the site. A beautiful sanctuary, it today bears none of the scars of the conquest. It is a place of worship that belongs to the people, and there are no echoes of tyranny. Within its soaring vault, in a space illuminated by candles and the light of pale Andean skies, I once stood at the altar, a newborn child in my arms, a boy swaddled in white linen, as an itinerant priest dripped holy water onto his forehead and spoke words of blessing that brought the infant into the realm of the saved. After the baptism, there was a celebration, and the child's parents, my new *compadres*, toasted every hopeful possibility. I too made promises, which in the ensuing years I attempted to fulfill. I had no illusions about the economic foundation of the bond. From me, my *compadres* hoped to secure support: in time, money for my godchild's education, perhaps the odd gift, a cow for the family, a measure of security in an uncertain nation. From them, I wanted nothing but the chance to know their world, an asset far more valuable than anything I could offer.

This pact, never spoken about and never forgotten, was, in its own way, a perfect reflection of the Andes, where the foundation of all life, both today and in the time of the Inca, has always been reciprocity. One sees it in the fields, where men come together and work in teams, moving between rows of fava beans and potatoes, season to season, a day for a day, planting, hoeing, weeding, mounding, harvesting. There is a spiritual exchange in the morning when the first of a family to awake salutes the sun, and again at the end of the day when a father returning from the fields whispers prayers of thanksgiving and lights a candle before greeting his family. Every offering is a gift: blossoms scattered onto fertile fields, the blessing of the children and tools at the end of each day, coca leaves presented to Pachamama at any given moment. When people meet on a trail, they pause and exchange *k'intus* of coca, three perfect leaves aligned to form a cross. Turning to face the nearest *apu*, or mountain spirit, they bring the leaves to the mouth and blow softly, a ritual invocation that sends the essence of the plant back to the earth, the community, the sacred places, and the souls of the ancestors. The exchange of leaves is a social gesture, a way of acknowledging a human connection. But the blowing of the *phukuy*, as it is called, is an act of spiritual reciprocity, for in giving selflessly to the earth, the individual ensures that in time the energy of the coca will return full circle, as surely as rain falling on a field will inevitably be reborn as a cloud.

Almost twenty years after first visiting Chinchero, I returned to participate in an astonishing ritual, the *mujonomiento*, the annual running of the boundaries. Since the time of the Inca, the town has been divided into three *ayullus*, or communities, the most traditional of which is Cuper, the home of my *compadres*, and, to my mind, the most beautiful, for its lands encompass Antakillqa and all the soaring ridges that separate Chinchero from the sacred valley of the Urubamba. Within Cuper are four hamlets, and once each year, at the height of the rainy season, all the males, save those elders physically incapable of the feat, run the boundaries of their respective communities. It is a race but also a pilgrimage, for the frontiers are marked by mounds of earth, holy sites where prayers are uttered and ritual gestures lay claim to the land. The distance travelled by the members of each hamlet varies. The track I was to follow, that of Pucamarca, covers some fifteen miles, but the route crosses two Andean ridges, dropping a thousand feet from the plaza of Chinchero to the base of Antakillqa, then ascending three thousand feet to a summit spur before descending to the valley on the far side, only to climb once more to reach the grasslands of the high *puna* and the long trail home.

At the head of each contingent would dart the *waylaka*, the strongest and fleetest of the youths, transformed for the day from male to female. Dressed in heavy woollen skirts and a cloak of indigo, wearing a woman's hat and delicate lace, the *waylaka* would fly up the ridges, white banner in hand. At every boundary marker, the transvestite had to dance, a rhythmic turn that like a vortex would draw to the peaks the energy of the women left behind in the villages far below. Each of the four hamlets of Cuper has its own trajectory, just as each of the three *ayullus* has its own land to traverse. By the end of the day, all of Chinchero would be reclaimed: the rich plains and verdant fields of Ayullupunqu; the lakes, waterfalls, mountains, and cliffs of Cuper; the gorges of Yanacona, where wild things thrive and rushing streams carry away the rains to the Urubamba. Adversaries would have been fought, spirits invoked, a landscape defined, and the future secured.

This much I knew as I approached the plaza on the morning of the event. Before dawn, the blowing of the conch shells had awoken the town, and the *waylakas*, once dressed, had walked from house to house, saluting the various authorities: the *curaca* and *alcalde*; the officers of the church; and the *embarados*, those charged with the preservation of tradition. At each threshold, coca had been exchanged, fermented maize *chicha* imbibed, and a cross of flowers hung in reverence above the doorway. For two hours, the procession had moved from door to door, musicians in tow, until it encompassed all of the community and drew everyone in celebration to the plaza, where women waited, food in hand: baskets of potatoes and spicy *piquante*, flasks of *chicha*, and steaming plates of vegetables. There I lingered, with gifts of coca for all. At my side was my godson, Armando. A grown man now, father of an infant girl, he had been a tailor but worked now in the markets of Cusco, delivering sacks of potatoes on a tricycle rented from a cousin. He had returned to Chinchero to be with me for the day.

What I could never have anticipated was the excitement and the rush of adrenaline, the sensation of imminent flight as the entire assembly of men, prompted by some unspoken signal, began to surge toward the end of the plaza. With a shout, the *waylaka* sprang down through the ruins, carrying with him more than a hundred runners and dozens of young boys who scattered across the slopes that funnelled downward toward a narrow dirt track. The trail fell away through a copse of eucalyptus and passed along the banks of a creek that dropped to the valley floor. A mile or two on, the *waylaka* paused for an instant, took measure of the men, caught his breath, and was off, dashing through thickets of buddleja and polylepis as the rest of us scrambled to keep sight of his white banner. Crossing the creek draw, we moved up the face of Antakillqa. Here at last the pace slowed to something less than a full run. Still, the men leaned into the slope with an intensity and determination unlike anything I had ever seen before. Less than two hours after leaving the village, we reached the summit ridge, a climb of several thousand feet.

There we paused, as the *waylaka* planted his banner atop a *mujon*, a tall mound of dirt, the first of the border markers. The authorities added their ceremonial staffs, and as the men piled on dirt to augment the size of the *mujon*, Don Jeronimo, the *curaca*, sang rich invocations that broke into a cheer for the well-being of the entire community. By this point, the runners were as restless as racehorses, frantic to move. A salutation, a prayer, a generous farewell to those of Cuper Pueblo, another of the hamlets, who would track north, and we of Pucamarca were off, heading east across the backside of the mountain to a second *mujon* located on a dramatic promontory overlooking all of the Urubamba. Beyond the hamlets and farms of the sacred valley, clouds swirled across the flanks of even higher mountains, as great shafts of sunlight fell upon the river and the fields far below.

We pounded on across the backside of the mountain and then

straight down at a full run through dense tufts of *ichu* grass and
meadows of lupine and rue. Another *mujon*, more prayers, handfuls of
coca all around, blessings and shouts, and a mad dash off the mountain to the valley floor, where, mercifully, we older men rested for a
few minutes in the courtyard of a farmstead owned by a beautiful old
woman who greeted us with a great ceramic urn of frothy *chicha*. One
of the authorities withdrew from his pocket a sheet of paper listing
the names of the men and began to take attendance. Participation in
the *mujonomiento* is obligatory, and those who fail to appear must pay
a fine to the community. As the names were called, I glanced up and
was stunned to see the *waylaka*, silhouetted on the skyline hundreds
of feet above us, banner in hand, moving on.

So the day went. The rains began in early afternoon, and the
winds blew fiercely by four. By then nothing mattered but the energy
of the group, the trail at our feet, and the distant slope of yet another
ridge to climb. Warmed by alcohol and coca leaves, the runners fell
into reverie, a curious state of joy and release, almost like a trance.

Darkness was upon us as we rushed down the final canyon on a
broad muddy track where the streams of water ran together like
mercury and disappeared beneath the stones. Approaching the valley
floor and the hamlet of Cuper Alto, where women and children
waited, the rain-soaked runners closed ranks behind the *waylaka* to
emerge from the mountains as a single force, an entire community
that had affirmed through ritual its sense of place and belonging. In
making the sacrifice, the men had reclaimed a birthright and ren-
dered sacred a homeland. Once reunited with their families, they
drank and sang, toasting their good fortune as the women served
great steaming bowls of soup from iron cauldrons. And, of course,
late into night, the *waylakas* danced.

THIS MOVEMENT THROUGH LANDSCAPE, the *mujonomiento*, with its obligations and social engagement, reveals the role that ritual plays in forging the bonds of memory that define a people's sense of place and belonging. It also shows the importance of embracing metaphor as we attempt to understand traditional relationships to land, history, community, and the spirit realm. Ultimately, this is our great challenge. How do those of us who have grown so distant from the soil and the mystic threads of recollection that gave rise to our being explain the wonder of those peoples who still engage the land? Most of our popular explanations come up short. Many still invoke Rousseau, implying that indigenous peoples are by nature closer to the land than we can possibly be, not only a silly idea but one that is racist in its simplicity. Others recall Thoreau, suggesting that indigenous peoples are more conscious of and contemplative about their place in nature than those of us born into the industrial world.

Indigenous peoples are neither sentimental nor nostalgic. Life in the malarial swamps of New Guinea, the chill winds of Tibet, the white heat of the Sahara leaves little room for sentiment. Nostalgia is not commonly associated with Inuit. Nomadic hunters and gatherers in Borneo have no conscious sense of stewardship for mountain forests that they lack the technical ability to destroy. What these cultures have done, however, is to forge through time and ritual a traditional mystique of Earth that is based not only on deep attachment to the land but also on a far more subtle intuition—the idea that the land itself is breathed into being by human consciousness. Mountains, rivers, and forests are not perceived as inanimate, as mere props on a stage upon which the human drama unfolds. For these societies, the land is alive, a dynamic force to be embraced and transformed by the human imagination. Here lies the essence of the relationship between indigenous peoples and the natural world.

But what does this belief mean in practice, and how does the conviction become manifest in the world? The young lad in Chinchero, honoured as a *waylaka* and raised to believe that a mountain is the abode of a protective spirit, will be a profoundly different human being from a youth brought up to believe that a mountain is an inert mass of rock ready to be mined. A Kwakwaka'wakw boy raised to revere the coastal forests of the Pacific Northwest as the abode of Huxwhukw and the Crooked Beak of Heaven, cannibal spirits living at the north end of the world, will be a different person from a Canadian child taught to believe that such forests exist to be logged.

Is the mountain a sacred place? Do spirits walk the coastal forests of Canada? Does a river follow the ancestral path of an anaconda? Was Jesus the Son of God, a man capable of walking on water, raising the dead, transforming a single fish into food for the multitudes? Who is to say? What matters is the potency of the belief and the manner in which the conviction plays out in the day-to-day life of a people.

All beliefs are suspect, of course, and few societies realize in practice the full promise and demands of their formal convictions. All peoples acknowledge the chasm that invariably exists between societal ideals and the reality of daily life and practice. Ultimately what matters is not how closely a people follows a set of rules but rather what those rules say about how those people perceive their place in the world. The full measure of a culture embraces both the actions of its people and the quality of their aspirations, the character and nature of the metaphors that propel them onward. Thus the significance of an esoteric belief lies not in its veracity in some absolute sense but in what it can tell us about a culture.

Ten thousand years ago, the Neolithic revolution transformed human destiny; with agriculture came surplus, specialization, hierarchy, and a religious worldview that replaced the poetry of the shaman with the prose of the institutional priesthood. Three hundred years ago, at the dawn of the industrial age, the spirit of the Enlightenment liberated the individual from the constraints of community. This was an even more profound innovation, the sociological equivalent of the splitting of the atom. Still, in much of the world, neither innovation took hold. In Australia, the Aboriginal peoples neither freed the individual nor succumbed to the cult of progress. For thousands of years, they travelled lightly on the land. To be sure, they set fire to grasslands and forest, killed what game they could. But for the most part, their impact on their environment was nominal. Why were they exempt from the impulses to improve on the wild that propelled our ancestors? An explanation may be found in the fundamental beliefs that defined their existence.

The Europeans who colonized Australia were unprepared for the sophistication of the place and its inhabitants, incapable of embracing its wonder. They had no understanding of the challenges of the desert and little sensitivity to the achievements of Aboriginal peoples who for over sixty thousand years had thrived as nomads, wanderers on a pristine continent. In all that time, the desire to improve upon the natural world, to tame the rhythm of the wild, had never touched them. The Aborigines accepted life as it was, a cosmological whole, the unchanging creation of the first dawn, when Earth and sky separated, and the original Ancestor brought into being all the primordial

Ancestors, who, through their thoughts, dreams, and journeys, sang the world into existence.

The Ancestors walked as they sang, and when it was time to stop, they slept. In their dreams, they conceived the events of the following day, points of creation that fused one into another until every creature, every stream and stone, all time and space became part of the whole, the divine manifestation of the one great seminal impulse. When they grew exhausted from their labours, they retired into the earth, sky, clouds, rivers, lakes, plants, and animals of an island continent that resonates with their memory. The paths taken by the Ancestors have never been forgotten. They are the Songlines, precise itineraries followed even today as the people travel across the template of the physical world.

As the Aborigines track the Songlines and chant the stories of the first dawning, they become part of the Ancestors and enter the Dreamtime, which is neither a dream nor a measure of the passage of time. It is the very realm of the Ancestors, a parallel universe where the ordinary laws of time, space, and motion do not apply, where past, future, and present merge into one. It is a place that Europeans can only approximate in sleep, and thus it became known to the early English settlers as the Dreaming, or Dreamtime. But the term is misleading. A dream by Western definition is a state of consciousness divorced from the real world. The Dreamtime, by contrast, is the real world, or at least one of two realities the Aborigines experience in their daily lives.

To walk the Songlines is to become part of the continuing creation of the world, a place that both exists and is still being formed. Thus, the Aborigines are not merely attached to Earth; they are essential to its existence. Without the land, they would die. But without the people, the process of creation would cease and Earth would wither. Through movement and sacred rituals, the people maintain access to the Dreamtime and play a dynamic and ongoing role in the world of the Ancestors.

A moment begins with nothing. A man or a woman walks, and from emptiness emerge the songs, the musical embodiment of reality, the cosmic melodies that give the world its character. The songs create vibrations that take shape. Dancing brings definition to the forms, and objects of the phenomenological realm appear: trees, rocks, streams, all of them physical evidence of the Dreaming. Should the rituals stop, the voices fall silent, all would be lost. For everything on Earth is held together by the Songlines, everything is subordinate to the Dreaming, which is constant but ever changing. Every landmark is wedded to a memory of its origins and yet is always being born. Every animal and object resonates with the pulse of an ancient event while still being dreamed into being. The world as it exists is perfect, though it is constantly being formed. The land is encoded with everything that ever has been, everything that ever will be, in every dimension of reality. To walk the land is to engage in a constant act of affirmation, an endless dance of creation.

The Europeans who first washed ashore on the beaches of Australia lacked the language or imagination even to begin to understand the profound intellectual and spiritual achievements of the Aborigines. What they saw was a people who lived simply, whose technological achievements were modest, whose faces looked strange, whose habits were incomprehensible. The Aborigines lacked all the hallmarks of European civilization. They had no metal tools, knew nothing of writing, had never succumbed to the cult of the seed. Without agriculture or animal husbandry, they generated no surpluses and thus never embraced sedentary village life. Hierarchy and specialization were unknown. Their small semi-nomadic bands, living in temporary shelters made of sticks and grass, dependent on stone weapons, epitomized European notions of backwardness. An early French explorer described them as "the most miserable people of the world, human beings who approach closest to brute beasts." As late as 1902, a member of the Australian parliament claimed, "There is no scientific evidence that the Aborigine is a human at all."

By the 1930s, a combination of disease, exploitation, and murder had reduced the Aborigine population from well over a million at the time of European contact to a mere thirty thousand. In one century, a land bound by Songlines, where the people moved effortlessly from one dimension to the next, from the future to the past and from the past to the present, was transformed from Eden to Armageddon. In light of what we know today of the extraordinary reach of the Aboriginal mind, the subtlety of Aboriginal thoughts, and the evocative power of Aboriginal rituals, it is chilling to think that this reservoir of human potential, wisdom, intuition, and insight very nearly ran dry during those terrible years of death and conflagration. As it is, Aboriginal languages, which may have numbered 250 at the time of contact, are disappearing at the rate of 1 or more a year. Only 18 are spoken today by as many as 500 individuals.

Despite this history, the Aborigines have survived and, in time, may still have a chance to inspire and redeem a nation. But what of the other victims of conquest, the untold scores of nations driven out of existence by forces beyond their capacity to engage and overcome?

FOR AT LEAST TEN THOUSAND YEARS, the San Bushmen have occupied the sandveld regions of Botswana, Namibia, and southern Angola. Numbering perhaps 55,000, they are the descendants of a people who inhabited the entire subcontinent and much of East Africa thousands of years before the arrival of either black or white pastoralists and farmers. Unlike the agriculturists who spread inexorably across the land, transforming the wild and constantly moving onward, the nomadic San essentially stayed put, subsisting as hunters and gatherers in a seasonal round that left little mark on Earth. Like the Aboriginal peoples of Australia, they accepted the world as it was. Rather than struggle with the natural world, they moved to its rhythm, not out of conviction, but because their survival depended upon doing so. Thus they adapted to one of the most extreme landscapes on the planet.

Water is the great challenge. For ten months of the year there is none, at least on the surface of the ground. In the past the San sought moisture in the hollows of trees, used reeds to suck it out of sipwells beneath the mud, or resorted to hidden supplies, cached in ostrich eggs buried beneath the sand and marked with the insignia of the owner. For most of the year, there is no water at all, and the people traditionally depended totally on melons and tubers and whatever liquid could be squeezed from the guts of prey. To replenish the three quarts of moisture lost each day through perspiration, the San had to consume twelve pounds of wild melon. With the onset of the dry season in May, the melons shrivelled and the people were forced to dig for tubers deep within the sand. Throughout the year plants provided 80 per cent of their food and 90 per cent of their water. The possibility of dying of thirst was a constant.

By September, the season of the Brown Hyena, the time of greatest privation, the San spent their days lying still in shallow hollows moistened with urine, tormented by clouds of flies and tortured by the withering heat. October marks the beginning of the Little Rains, teasing raindrops that touch the Earth but do little to relieve the drought. The heat continues. High winds sweep over the burnt grasslands and the spirits of the dead appear in the shape of dust devils, dancing across a grey-and-yellow landscape. Finally, in January, the rains return, and the next three months are a time of rebirth and regeneration. Some years great rolling clouds break open to flood the desert with thunderous downpours, inches of precious water forming silver sheets upon the desert. Some years it does not rain at all.

The rainy season, from January to March, is a time of relative abundance. People move about the desert in small extended-family groups, harvesting seeds and fruit, rejoicing to find standing pools of water or hives of bees with rare offerings of honey, a sublime delicacy for a people whose diet for much of the year consists of fibrous roots and bitter tubers. April brings yet another change, a short autumn, the season of the hunter. This is the San's favourite time of year. The rains have driven away the heat, and the cold of winter has yet to descend. There is ripe food everywhere and the animals are fat.

Although the San depend largely on plants for their food, it is hunting that defines them as a people. From family encampments the men range across the desert in small hunting parties of three or four, covering as much as twenty miles in a day, returning by night, only to hunt again with the dawn. They carry just their weapons and a few essentials—a short bow and a quiver of arrows, fire-making tools, a hollow reed for sipping water from the sand, perhaps a knife, a short spear, a lump of gum or resin to make repairs. Moving in teams, they read the ground for signs. Nothing is overlooked—a trodden blade of grass, the direction of a tear in a leaf, the depth and shape of a track. Legendary stalkers, the San can distinguish and follow the sign of a single wounded animal though it moves in a herd of thousands. Every human footprint has a name, for the San recognize a person's mark with the precision of a forensic expert linking a fingerprint to a suspect.

Everything is hunted. Hippos die in pits lined with poisoned poles. Elephants are brought down with the blow of an ax to the hamstring. Lions sluggish from gorging on meat are chased from a kill. Antelope are run to the ground. Birds are snared in nets woven from desert fibres. The hunting gear is primitive—spears and small arrows of limited range. The key to success lies in the San's knowledge of the prey and of the plants and beetle grubs that, properly prepared, yield the most lethal of poisons so that the slightest wound results in convulsions, paralysis, and death.

From the desert adaptation emerges a way of life. Nothing is wasted, least of all one's own energy. In the heat of midday, people remain still. Taboos reserve certain foods for the weak and elderly, tortoise and ostrich eggs and creatures, such as snakes, that are readily found and killed. All food is shared. To refuse a gift is an act of unforgivable hostility. To accept is to acknowledge one's place in a community of life.

For the San, who never stay long in one place and yet never travel far from the land of their birth, the centre of social life is the encampment and the sacred fire that burns at its heart. For these desert people the sun is not a sign of life but a symbol of death. Life is found in the family hearth, the fire that brings warmth in the night and provides shelter in the darkness. A mother gives birth in the shadows and returns to the fire. When a marriage fails, a young girl slips away and heads home to her father's fire. An elder no longer capable of keeping up with his group is left behind to die, a circle of brush built around him to keep back the hyenas, a fire at his feet to lead him on to the next world. To placate the God of the West, the spirits of the dead, and all the forces of evil, the San dance, spinning around the fire in trance, placing their heads in the burning coals, as the energy moves up their spines, touching the base of their skulls and diffusing through their bodies and into the earth itself. Whenever trouble threatens, the San kindle a fire and find solace and protection in the flames.

Today it would take a conflagration to save the San Bushmen. War and dislocation, disease and hunger now stalk their encampments, which have become oases of dependency in the barren sands of South Africa. Within a generation they have been forced from their lands. Alcohol has numbed the senses of too many trackers. Mothers work as servants and prostitutes as their children grow old on a diet of maize gruel imported from abroad. AIDS is rampant, and young men who have never brought down an antelope confront death daily.

Like so many indigenous peoples, the San Bushmen have suffered immensely in the past fifty years. But their loss is also ours. The real measure of an individual or a people emerges in times of stress and crisis. Similarly, the full wonder of the human imagination and spirit is often most powerfully revealed by cultures that confront and overcome extraordinary challenges and vicissitudes. It is one thing, for example, to craft a culture from the fertile soils of the Nile delta. It is quite another to find a way to survive and thrive in the barren reaches of the Kalahari. There can be no better sign of genius than the ability to track game in a dust storm, to draw venom from the larvae of a beetle, to smell and find moisture three feet beneath the searing sands of a desert.

Just as the death of a visionary tracker impoverishes us all, so too the disappearance of an ancient way of life, morally inspired and inherently right, represents a loss to all humanity. For each culture is a unique facet of the human imagination, and together the myriad peoples of the world comprise the repertoire with which we will all chart a way through the next centuries. This perhaps is why I tell these stories, with the hope that somehow we will come to understand that these peoples are divine manifestations of the spirit and that they, as much as we, hold the keys to our cultural survival.

DIANE ACKERMAN

The Deer in Springtime

Poet, essayist, and naturalist DIANE ACKERMAN has published numerous books of poetry and nonfiction and has taught at a variety of universities. Her nonfiction includes Cultivating Delight; The Rarest of the Rare, in which she explores the plight and fascination of endangered animals; and the bestseller A Natural History of the Senses. Her essays about nature and human nature have appeared in many journals, including National Geographic and the New Yorker. She also has the rare distinction of having a molecule named after her (dianeackerone).

In the very earliest time,
when both people and animals lived on earth,
a person could become an animal if he wanted to
and an animal could become a human being.
Sometimes they were people
and sometimes they were animals
and there was no difference.
All spoke the same language.
That was the time when words were like magic.
The human mind had mysterious powers.
A word spoken by chance
might have strange consequences.
It would suddenly come alive
and what people wanted to happen could happen—
all you had to do was say it.
Nobody could explain this.

—Anonymous Inuit poem

ONE DAY, WHEN THE LAST snows have melted, the air tastes tinny and sweet for the first time in many months. That subtle tincture of new buds, sap, and loam I've learned to recognize as the first whiff of springtime. Suddenly a brown shape moves in the woods, then blasts into sight as it clears the fence at the bottom of the yard. A beautiful doe with russet flanks and nimble legs, she looks straight at me as I watch from the living-room window; then she drops her gaze.

Like fireworks, five more deer make equally spectacular leaps and land squarely on the grass. But once they touch earth all their buoyancy seems to vanish, and they lumber around the yard, droopy, gaunt, exhausted. A big doe lifts a hind foot to scratch her shaggy cheek. I think that's the doe I named Triangle last year, because of a geometrical pattern in her coat. But, at the moment, the deer are in moult, which must feel itchy; and since they don't shed evenly, their usually sleek coats look crisscrossed by small weather systems.

Mainly the deer seem frantic with hunger. They start eating the dried-up lavender leaves, whose pungent smell usually keeps them at bay. They've lost their winter fat, but there's nothing in bloom. Their living larder won't be full for weeks. Desperate, they devour the bittersweet and pull bark from aspens and other trees they don't prefer. In summer's banquet, they can afford to be sloppy and eat whatever they fancy. Now, searching for the highest-protein foods, they hunt carefully among the garden's leftovers.

I love watching the deer, which always arrive like magic or miracle or the answer to an unasked question. Can there be a benediction of deer on a chilly spring morning? I think so. Their otherworldliness stops the day in its tracks, focuses it on the hypnotic beauty of nature, and then starts the day again with a rush of wonder. There is a way of sitting quietly and beholding nature that is a form of meditation or prayer, and like those healing acts it calms the spirit.

Come summer, of course, the deer will ransack my herb garden, plunder my roses, and destroy the raised beds, leaving their footprints as calling cards among the decapitated flowers. They are terrorists in the garden. That's why I've planted most of my roses in a special fenced-in garden with a solid gate.

It feels a little odd, being in competition with deer, but that's what comes of cultivating so much land. If we replace their vegetation with buildings and crops, we leave the deer no choice but to raid our gardens. And humans have been known to raid deer, even cultivate them as a crop. For millennia, Chinese herbals have included deer parts, favouring antler velvet, bone marrow, spinal cord, penis, undigested milk, fetus, brains, thyroid gland, and much more as remedies. If human beings were not sitting smugly atop the food chain, what curios of our bodies would other species use as medicines? A thought explored in gory detail by many science fiction books and movies.

These deer are beautiful and whole, not a sum of their parts, and I'm happy to share everything but prize flowers with them. But how to protect those flowers? Friends sometimes recommend such deer deterrents as bags of hair from a barbershop, used tampons, cougar pee, mothballs, salsa, bars of smelly soap, and barking dogs. I find that an oily soap called Hinder works reasonably well and won't harm child or animal, but you have to spray it after every rainfall. This year I finally hit on a solution: pinwheels. I planted one beside each treasured bush or flower. Spinning randomly and sparkling in the sun, they seem alive and so the deer avoid them. I also like how festive the pinwheels look decorating the garden with colour and motion and the soft whir of their blades

But I leave all the apples from both trees just for the deer, I let them eat their fill from the raspberry vines, and I feed them in hard weather. Sometimes in colder months I leave apples beneath the twin apple trees, where deer would expect to find them. For a decade, the apple trees have helped the deer survive winter. What with the changing current of El Niño and several volcanoes hurling dust high into the atmosphere, the apple trees were sparse this year and the deer found few apples beneath the snow. Despite thick, burro-like coats, they looked thin. I suppose I am "conflicted" about the deer, as psychological folk like to say. But mainly I am grateful to have these emissaries of the wild so close at hand, and when they visit all I can manage is praise.

We've worked hard to exile ourselves from nature; yet we end up longing for what we've lost: a sense of connectedness. I've been watching the deer and other animals with affectionate curiosity through many seasons. Their distresses echo the ones I see among my neighbours; their triumphs teach me about the indomitableness of life. For many homeowners, suburbanites, and travellers, backyard animals such as deer, squirrels, birds, and raccoons become an entryway to the bustling world of nature. Studying animals is easy when they're nearby, and there's nothing like the thrill of recognizing individual animals with unique looks and personalities. The doe with the white half-circle beneath one eye, who stands up on her rear legs to pick apples off the trees, the young buck who always does a small war dance before he leaps a fence. When that happens, we lose our "us against them" attitude and start to feel part of a kingdom of neighbours. Deep in our instincts and cells we remember living wild in nature, fitting into the seamless circle of the seasons, reading the weather and landscape, facing frights and challenges. In a real sense we now are out of our element, and it's small wonder we relish rare visits to nature—picnics, jogs, and bike rides; journeys to parks, campgrounds, and zoos.

Faced with human-wrought catastrophes, we are tempted to

banish concerns about nature to the edge of our awareness. But there will always be important reasons to care, some of them moral, some practical. For instance, one might argue that it's our moral duty, as citizens of the planet, to protect its treasures. There are also good selfish reasons—the vanishing rain forests contain pharmaceuticals we might want or need to survive; the Antarctic holds drinking water; thick forests ensure that we have enough oxygen to breathe. But another reason is older and less tangible. We require a lively bustling natural world, without whose intimate truths we can find ourselves unravelling.

We may feel cozy and safe in our homes, protected from both blast and predator, but we pay the price with slack muscles, weak hearts, and glum spirits. Deprived of daylight, we sink low during winter months. And yet when we search for remedies to those distresses, only the artifical spring to mind: gyms, pills, light boxes. By retreating farther and farther from nature, we lose our sense of belonging, suffer a terrible loneliness we can't name, and end up depriving ourselves of what we need to feel healthy and whole. Children know that instinctively, and when a tree stump or marsh beckons, they dive in, wide-eyed, all hands.

I suppose what we fear is loss of control, of ourselves and of our planet; and there's no doubt, nature is chaotic, random, violent, uncontainable, no matter how hard we try to outwit it. But it's also dazzling, soothing, all-embracing, and restorative. Wonder is a bulky emotion; when it fills the heart and mind there's little room for anything else. We need the intimate truths of daylight and deer.

Deer are such a panic species that the only way to be among them without frightening them is to hunker down low and positively not look. Eye contact, even glancing, may distress them. Most often, wild animals make eye contact only when they wish to fight, eat, or mate. If you seem to be ignoring them, you pose little threat. And so I steal out, bent low, carrying a sliced-up peach I place on the grass near the apple trees; then, still without making eye contact, I creep back indoors. Soon two deer sniff their way to the treasure, so unfamiliar yet so sweet, and stand eating with peach juice dripping from their mouths. Squirrels seem comforted by the sound of my voice when I'm among them, but deer require silence.

One noon last summer, I saw two fawns sitting on the grass in the shade of a large tree in my front yard. Quietly I crept out with concealed purpose—I walked easily across the yard, as if on an errand unrelated to the deer. Because I seemed preoccupied by human things, they watched me, ever alert, but didn't bother to stir as I sat down in the grass near them, averting my eyes, picking a blade of grass or two, only now and then studying them with long, thick glances. A passing car startled them and they half stood, then settled down again. Deer don't fold their legs like dogs but slide down over the tops of their knees like camels. As I continued my mock grazing, they curled up and snoozed.

Where was their mother, and wasn't she afraid to leave them alone among humans? Typically, a doe will have one or two fawns and hide them in a secluded spot while she forages, returning only to nurse them. During the first few weeks of life, fawns don't give off much scent. Small, quiet, camouflaged, and nearly odourless, they're not easily discovered, so Mother may drift off without much concern. Or I might well have been in her sights and dismissed as another creature out grazing in the sun. Humans are familiars to suburban deer.

By midsummer the fawns were subsisting on a vegetarian diet that included hundreds of species of buds and leaves, and they were roaming a wide area. They left scent clouds in the forest. Late in the day, I would often see them wander into open areas to nibble broad-leafed plants and watch them position themselves downwind, slowly roaming upwind, always alert for the smell of predators. Deer tend to twitch their tails just before lifting their heads, so whenever I see the tail-twitch, I stand still and drop my eyes. If I scare them, they'll pronk away in an awkward, tail-flashing pantomime that says, "I know you see me, but I'm too fast for you! Too strong for you! It's no use chasing me!" To my mind, prey calling attention to itself as a bluff seems dicey, but apparently gazelles do the same thing.

Now, nearly a year later, the fawns are grown, their speckles have disappeared, and their bellies look gaunt. The lovely reddish-brown coats they wore as gawky juveniles have been replaced by the sombre greyish-brown of adulthood. These coats are more loosely woven, but each hair is hollow so that trapped air will heat up like a comforter on chilly nights. I cannot tell if they're male or female. Not from a distance, anyway. Their mother is young, so most likely the fawns are females, which deer tend to produce early in their breeding life. Later on, as a doe ages, it's advantageous to have males and fuss over them, suckling them longer, making sure they grow strong, so that her genes will flourish as they grow to best their rivals and dominate harems. Many animals are able instinctively to choose the sex of their off-spring. Do humans make such unconscious choices? I wonder.

Remembering what I was saving for the squirrel and bird feeders, I grab a jacket and hurry into the garage, returning with six ears of corn and the utility apples I was saving for a pie. Then, slipping slowly out back, I toss the corn across the yard. The deer stare squarely at it from a distance, tentatively approach the corn, realize what it is, and eagerly begin to gnaw one cob apiece. As I toss apples to the largest female, she regards me solidly, eye to eye. An apple lands a yard in front of her, and still she watches me carefully, then walks toward the apple, slices it with one bite, and eats with a mixture of surprise and relish. Apples in April! She looks back at me, allows me to settle low on my haunches and watch her and her family. I try not to move.

In time, she wanders toward the others, also happily eating apples and corn. The deer will survive at least one more day because of this food, maybe a few days, maybe long enough to get to the next decent meal. Knowing that, I feel my heart lighten. It is a moment sealed in a glass paperweight, a scene to be reflected in a gazing ball, a time of peaceful communion with nature. And there I sit on the grass until evening drops a grey screen over the air and daylight drains away.

At last the deer become startled by something real or imaginary and trot back toward the woods, the largest doe leading the way along the fence. When she finds a place she feels comfortable with, she lines up squarely and hurdles it. The others pace nervously. One stands before the fence, lifts a foot as if to jump, thinks about it again, backs up, paces, once more aborts the attempt, and finally risks it: a from-standing-still five-foot jump straight up. Her hoofs graze the top rail as she clears it. Over the years, the deer have bent the fence low between us. Soon the others follow, launching themselves from the tidy world of humans back into their familiar pandemonium of green.

TIMOTHY FINDLEY

Space and Time Enough

After an international career as an actor, TIMOTHY FINDLEY *came to prominence as a writer with his 1977 novel,* The Wars, *winner of a Governor General's Award and now a Canadian classic. He has received numerous other awards and honorary doctorates. His other novels include* Famous Last Words, *the award-winning* Not Wanted on the Voyage, *and his most recent,* Spadework. *His work as a playwright includes* The Stillborn Lover *and* Elizabeth Rex, *which also received a Governor General's Award. Timothy Findley died in Provence in June 2002. This essay was his final piece of writing.*

I AM NOT A SCIENTIST. I am a fiction writer—a storyteller. In some ways, the two disciplines are not all that different. We both seek meaning and understanding in what we explore. Where we differ is in method. Although we both ask *when*, the scientist also asks *what* and *how*, while the fiction writer asks *who* and *why*.

Two of the greatest subjects of every kind of investigation are time and space, but whereas exploratory travel in space is constantly being extended (some might say overextended) by science, the ability to travel in time is so far restricted to fiction.

Our common experience, however, is that anyone can journey through both space and time—at least in some senses. This is what I have noticed in my wanderings across my own country, as I have gone from the densely populated, highly developed area of my birth in Ontario to the more open, relatively untouched stretches of the West and the North. In many instances, it was like time-travelling into the past. And sometimes there were hints, as well, about the future.

Let me tell you about two such journeys I made with my companion, Bill Whitehead, a former biologist and science writer. Each time, we eventually headed farther north than we had ever been. What follows is not the complete story of our travels but the story of who we are and where we live.

By the summer of 1969, we had been working very hard for seven years; we were two ex-actors, trying to establish ourselves as writers—me on the page, Bill on the television screen. We had been successful enough to have saved up some money and decided to buy a kayak and a tent, take a summer off, and explore part of what is now Nunavut but was then known as the Northwest Territories.

The previous months had been so filled with work, we decided to begin our journey with a restful detour to the coast of Maine, following my family's tradition of holidaying in an old seaside hotel, the Atlantic House, where my father had been taken, aged two, in his father's arms in 1905.

The hotel had opened in the 1850s and had changed very little since then. Apart from the sleek shapes of the cars in the parking lot and the relative skimpiness of the bathing "costumes" on the beach, it was almost as if we had gone back into the nineteenth century and were enjoying a Victorian sojourn by the sea. Sand—stones—pine trees—lobsters—corn on the cob—gauze curtains—simple beds—the smells of salt water, sun cream, and wine. Privilege. Of course, you can never completely escape the present, which is why I used the Atlantic House as the setting for a later murder mystery, *The Telling of Lies*.

After a week or so of soaking up the sun and feasting on seafood, we christened our kayak in the Atlantic's cold waves, packed everything up, and headed west.

Our first night on the road was spent in Crawford's Notch, Vermont—in the same public campground we had always used on the journey to and from Maine. And here too there was a sense of going back in time. The relative peacefulness of wilderness, little evidence of the twentieth century. All very pleasant. To my delight, my mentor, Thornton Wilder, mentioned Crawford's Notch in his play *Our Town*—albeit unhappily. Someone dies there. But . . . so it goes.

Then came our second night—in the Mohawk Valley of upper New York State. Here, the campground was a crazy parody of *Roughing It in the Bush*. While we were setting up the camp, a truck came along, delivering firewood. Then the ice truck, the beer truck, the grocery truck. Then the truck with loudspeakers, proclaiming the title of the movie to be shown that evening in the outdoor cinema. And after the movie, the huge and noisy audience streamed past, heading for the various luxurious RVs parked everywhere, each with its portable TV set. Then we saw the final ironic image of Campground U.S.A.: a woman in stiletto heels and Gucci toreador pants, flourishing a martini glass and accompanied by a shampooed miniature poodle. Ah, wilderness . . .

Fast-forward through the megapolitan wonders of Chicago and the corn-filled gridwork of Iowa's flatlands to the arid stretches of the Midwest. As we listened on the car radio to the reports of the first human landing on the moon, we were installed in a lunar landscape of our own—the Badlands of South Dakota. Was this barren panorama an image of the burgeoning exploration of space? Or of the coming desertification of our own verdant planet, worked to death by agro-biz?

We had set up camp in a Badlands park and, that evening, decided to attend one of the park's entertainment features. Members of a local native tribe would stage a program of traditional dances. The costumes were spectacular—and so were the dancers. The climax of the evening was, in a sense, a bonus. As one of the tribal elders, a woman, led the band in a rain dance, the sky darkened with storm clouds. Suddenly, a thunderous bolt of lightning announced the beginnings of a deluge. Everyone ran for shelter, the campers complaining as they headed for their tents, the dancers trying to stifle their laughter as they ran to their trucks.

We were lucky. Our tent withstood the storm. The one beside us was completely washed away by the torrential runoff—with no loss of life or limb, only of dignity. The whole experience brought to mind the various ways in which the human species has tried to achieve control over nature and how often—and how drastically—such attempts can backfire.

Within a few days, our westward push turned to the north, and two weeks later, we had left "civilization" behind. No more cities—just a few scattered towns and villages, connected by endless vistas of scrub forest and crushed-rock roads. The sense of distance—and of peacefulness—was wonderful.

It was an unforgettable time: days passing without sight of another human being, setting up camp beside wild lakes whose shores offered a deep, soft bed of mosses, sharing our meals with the ravens and Canada jays (we still refuse to call them grey jays) who came, unafraid, to join us at the table. Coming across a flock of sandhill cranes feeding along a woodland roadway, shortly after we had encountered the great beast we called Caesar—a wood buffalo bull, emerging from the trees with what resembled a laurel wreath wrapped around his horns. At night, we listened to spine-tingling wolf chorales—two packs, at least half a mile apart, singing to each other in the northern moonlight. Reaching the Mackenzie River, we bent to drink its unpolluted waters. Utter enchantment. And again, a hint of what the Canadian landscape once had to offer on a wider, more generous scale.

Finally, after almost two months of all this, we headed south, passing down the stepped tableland of northern Alberta with ever new vistas before us. It was somewhere north of Peace River that we began to pick up newscasts on our car radio. And what was the main item on the first report we heard? The ghastly story of Charles Manson and Sharon Tate in California. Welcome back to civilization!

If we still view our northern trip as a kind of idyll—a journey into what life in North America used to be—is this mere romanticism? An unrealistic yearning for a time that is largely lost in the past? Not completely. It remains, for us, a personal monument to the inexpressible wonders of wilderness and an irrefutable argument for preserving as much of it as possible. The human spirit can be nourished, restored, and challenged by wilderness. Otherwise, we wither and diminish.

In 1974, we returned to the North, this time to Yukon. We were sent on a reconnaissance by the Canadian Broadcasting Corporation—a survey of some of the routes used by the gold seekers of 1898. This was to be part of our research for writing a television series based on Berton's *Klondike*—the story of the great gold rush.

Another set of time travels to dramatize a vital aspect of Canadian history, but the Klondike series, sadly, would be stillborn—victim of some early drastic cutbacks in CBC budgets.

We took the train from Toronto to Prince Rupert, B.C. There we boarded the ferry that would carry us north to Skagway, Alaska. Our ship would follow the Inland Passage, a course that headed north past the Queen Charlotte Islands and then threaded its way through the lesser-known islands just off the coasts of British Columbia and Alaska.

It was early spring. As we proceeded north, the days grew longer. Evenings had a silvery quality to them that was unique in our experience. There was one totally magical moment of time travel, when the passage between islands was so narrow and so shallow that a pilot had to drop a weighted line over the side and call out the soundings as we inched forward. Suddenly, we were on a Mississippi riverboat, waiting for the familiar bit of nineteenth-century river slang that would signify two fathoms: "mark twain!" That was when a young musician, somewhere on the upper deck, took out his trumpet and began to play a Beatles piece, "Yesterday." Talk about theatre. Talk about significance.

The next morning, we witnessed something fascinating. For an hour or two, we had been anchored offshore, while a launch from one of the coastal settlements was unloading supplies for its isolated community. We joined those who had gathered on the decks to watch, but the most interesting sight was a young couple with a beehive. They told us they were planning to homestead in Alaska and had decided to take advantage of the stop to let their bees seek food on shore. They assured us that many of the insects had already returned and that the rest would be back before we were on the move again. Would we like to see the rest of their stock? We followed the couple below decks, to where their vehicle was parked. It was an old circus truck, temporary home to a cow and her bull calf, a pair of pigs, several chickens, two horses, and a dog. Bales of hay—sacks of grain (for feed as well as planting)—farm implements that seemed to belong to another century.

We viewed all this with mixed feelings. Was this another brave new world—or another lost wilderness, about to be transformed into real estate? It was a question we never managed to answer, but I was able to use the image of the beehive on the deck in a later novel, *Not Wanted on the Voyage*—a retelling of the story of Noah and the Great

Flood, of how, on the human voyage through time, we have so drastically mistreated our fellow passengers on this planetary ark—all the other species on earth, to say nothing of our fellow human beings.

Eventually, we reached Skagway and disembarked to prepare for our journey over the Chilkoot Pass and down the Yukon River to Dawson City.

Skagway was, in part, a tourist's version of time travel. Part of the town had been restored to its 1890s self, with boardwalks, saloons, and old hotels whose rooms featured turn-of-the-century beds and huge, lion-footed cast-iron bathtubs.

That first night, we sat at our window and watched as the silver light persisted on its way to dawn. Gradually, the human traffic on the street was replaced by a whole population of dogs. Everyone in Alaska, it seemed, owned several dogs—and at night, the canine citizens took over the town. We saw the chance encounters of friends, the gossiping, the visits paid to less fortunate acquaintances who were confined to fenced-in yards. It was an irresistible performance that kept us up for most of the night and that confirmed what a good survival strategy at least a few species had been granted in establishing such close relationships with humans.

In the morning, our survey party assembled on the shores of a small bay just north of town. To our amazement, the whole bay was alive with bald eagles. We gave up counting when we reached the sixties. Apparently there was a spawning run of small fish—a bonanza for eagles in the whole area. For us, it was an unprecedented image of plenty—and one rarely seen, now, in the south.

The trek to Dawson remains, in memory, a series of unforgotten freeze-frames: the startlingly pink toads we found among the lush ferns in the coastal rain forest; the heaps of bear dung, green and steaming with freshness; and soon, as the trees thinned out, the rocky interior blanketed with snow, while on the slopes above, white overhangs offered threats of avalanches.

As we laboured up the high, steep bank of rocks that leads to the Chilkoot Pass, we wondered at the perseverance of all those young men and women who flooded north, seeking their fortunes in the Yukon ground. Some found gold. Many found death. Fever. Starvation. We visited the Dawson graveyard, where roughly carved wooden signs bear Russian, Chinese, German, French, and North American names—and sadly young ages. We also visited the wasteland of mine tailings, relics of the later days when mechanization scraped out everything that digging by hand and panning could not reach. It was a vivid image of the impulse to force the earth to give up all its riches—no matter what devastation might be left behind.

When we had made it back to the coast and sailed south toward the train that would take us back to Ontario, we found that the coastal glaciers we had passed on our way up to Alaska were now melting into the Pacific. The mix of fresh and salt water produced a churn of nutrients and a resulting plankton bloom that was the first link in a bountiful food chain. There we saw killer whales plunging through the waves and could only guess at the massed populations of all sizes hidden beneath the sea's surface.

That was over a quarter of a century ago—and we have never gone back north. We are afraid of what we might find in development and loss of wilderness. Loss of the spirit of wilderness, with more people, more technology, and more pollution, to say nothing of the first signs of global shifting climates, disrupted plant and animal populations.

Now we hear that British Columbia's ban on offshore oil exploration may be lifted—that marine life along Canada's Pacific coast may soon be threatened by all the disturbances and accidents that such activity produces. Meanwhile, American oil and gas exploration is scheduled to begin in—of all places—a designated wildlife refuge in Alaska. Should we be surprised? I guess not.

Sad news, and just one more sign that we continue to ignore warnings—the warnings about the dangers of overpopulation, of the degradation of the environment, of depletion of nonrenewable resources, and of our ingrained reluctance to spend enough, now, for the development of alternative energy sources and better management of food stocks.

Too many people and not enough room to sustain so much human activity. Whether you view the world as a scientist, a writer of fiction, or a citizen of any stripe, it seems clear that not only are we running out of space, we are also running out of time. Our policies must become more enlightened before it is too late—before darkness engulfs us all.

Does thinking like this make me a pessimist? To paraphrase the answer Nadine Gordimer once gave to that same question: Would a pessimist take up a pen—and write?

The answer is no.

DAVID SUZUKI

Catching an Epiphany

DAVID SUZUKI *is a highly acclaimed geneticist and the host of*
The Nature of Things. *He has written numerous books,*
including Metamorphosis, Genethics *and* Wisdom of the
Elders *(both co-authored with Peter Knudtson),* The Sacred
Balance *(co-authored with Amanda McConnell), and* Good
News for a Change *(co-authored with Holly Dressel), and is*
the founder and chair of the David Suzuki Foundation.
He lives in Vancouver, British Columbia.

I WAS BORN IN VANCOUVER, BRITISH COLUMBIA, in 1936. My very first childhood memory is one of almost unbearable excitement—my father and I went to a store to buy a tent so that we could go camping. One of the salesmen set up a pup tent right there in the store, and Dad and I scrunched in and lay down together. Dad wrapped his arms around me and held me close as I squirmed in uncontrollable anticipation of our first camping trip.

My recollection of those early years in British Columbia is mostly snippets of memories around camping and fishing trips. On my very first fishing trip, at age four, we hiked in to Loon Lake, more a large pond than a lake, and while Dad fly-fished, I sat on the dock with a small rod and reel and a tin of manure worms, pulling in one small trout after another until I had my limit. I remember sitting in a rowboat as Dad trolled for sea-run cutthroats around Stanley Park; we also jigged for halibut off Spanish Banks, cast for sturgeon near the mouth of the Fraser River, and hiked up the Vedder River to catch steelhead and Dolly Varden.

Dad loved to take children fishing and turn them into avid anglers and outdoors people. His philosophy was to make sure a first-time fisher caught fish. Size didn't matter; it was the catching that hooked kids. To this day, adult strangers approach me to tell me how much they appreciated those fishing trips with Dad and how they are doing the same with their children and their friends. Throughout my childhood and adolescence, fishing continued to provide some of my most memorable experiences.

After the Japanese attack on Pearl Harbor, twenty thousand Japanese Canadians, most Canadian citizens by birth or naturalization, were rounded up under the iniquitous War Measures Act, which legitimizes the suspension of all rights of citizenship at times of ill-defined threat. So my Canadian-born parents and siblings and I were rounded up and shipped out of Vancouver with seventy-five pounds of luggage each. Dad was sent to a "road camp," where he worked on the Trans-Canada Highway, while my mother, my two sisters, and I were evacuated to the interior of British Columbia.

As a boy of six, I was shielded from the upheaval and my parents' distress, and everything seemed like a grand adventure. We went on a long train ride to be interned in an old ghost town that was a relic from a silver rush in the 1890s. I didn't go to school for a year because there were no facilities or teachers. We were squeezed into a tiny room in a decaying hotel crawling with bedbugs, where we shared toilets, cooking facilities, and baths that were so big I learned to swim in one. But none of this mattered to me because the internment camp that was to be home for three years was located in a magical place. We were at the end of a long, narrow lake—Slocan Lake—at the bottom of a valley whose western slopes would become Valhalla Provincial Park three decades later.

Without school to imprison me, I roamed the shores of the lake and rivers and the forests on the surrounding mountains like a young voyageur. The lake was filled with rainbow trout, whitefish, kokanee

(landlocked sockeye salmon), squawfish, suckers, and chubs, and I
fished for any of them indiscriminately.

By watching older boys and by trial-and-error, I learned to use
caddisfly larvae and helgramites as bait; I found that in early morning when the dew was still heavy, grasshoppers were stiff and torpid
and a cinch to catch. A year later when Dad joined us, we explored
the mountain creeks to fish for the abundant trout. In the camps,
Japanese internees were forbidden to fish, but to us fish were a staple
like rice and we carried on a cat-and-mouse relationship with the
authorities as we fished at every opportunity while trying to avoid
being caught. In those mountains, we encountered wolves, black
bears, coyotes, and porcupines; carefully avoided huge clumps of
spiny devil's club; and gathered bags of prized pine mushrooms (*mat-
sutake*) in the fall. This was biology as it should be learned, firsthand
in the wild, joyously and effortlessly.

As the end of the war approached, those Japanese-Canadian
families like mine who chose to remain in Canada were expelled
from British Columbia, and we ended up in Leamington, Canada's
southernmost town, on Lake Erie. This area of southern Ontario
was intensive farming country, flat fields with ditches running along
country roads and small wood lots on private property, a radically
different environment from British Columbia. But that very difference provided new opportunities for exploration. Spurred by Dad's
excitement about discovering entirely new species of fish and armed
with dip nets, my sisters and I investigated every ditch, creek, and
pond within biking range. We kept bottles of sunfish, small catfish,
baby turtles, and minnows. We fished for channel catfish, sheephead
(drum), silver bass, and smelt, each savoured for its distinctive taste
and texture. And we discovered Point Pelee, a jewel perched on the

southernmost tip of Canada. There the marshes were filled with birds, reptiles, insects, and fish, and the lakeshore was littered with fossils and dried carcasses of birds and fish. Point Pelee would later become a national park that is one of the most popular gathering places for birds and their watchers.

In 1949, we moved to London, Ontario, a city of seventy thousand people that was growing explosively and would increase fivefold in the next half a century. Yet even here there was much to fascinate me. My family had been wiped out financially by the evacuation, incarceration, and expulsion, so we gathered edible plants and caught fish to supplement our diet. Even though the Thames River ran right through the middle of London, it was a fabulous place to fish. I came to know every pool and riffle along a two-kilometre stretch near our house. There were plenty of black bass, carp, catfish, and suckers, and at certain times of the year, the river was jammed with spawning pike, silver bass, and pickerel. I learned where and how to catch frogs, crayfish, minnows, and leeches to use as bait.

Only a kilometre from our house was an immense swamp that held endless attractions. I was a loner. The war years had left me with an overriding sense of inferiority, and I anticipated rejection because I was Japanese. To make matters worse, my feeling of alienation was strongest just as I was in the throes of puberty. This was during an era when virginity was still prized, so it was impossible to do much about my sexual fantasies. That swamp was my salvation—all my hang-ups, fears, and frustrations fell away whenever I biked to that marsh. I was an avid insect collector, and the water was filled with bizarre creatures—whirligigs, water striders, and boatmen. It was in that enchanted place that I first spotted a bittern with its beak pointing straight up, trying to blend in with the surrounding reeds. And each spring, the swamp reverberated with the sexual calls of frogs that proved irresistible to mates and me. I'd return home triumphantly carrying jars of salamander and frog eggs that I could then watch metamorphose into tadpoles.

My father's enthusiastic embrace of new fishing places and species had shown me there were worlds to be experienced wherever one lived, and I found that to be true when I finished high school and moved from Ontario to Massachusetts, Illinois, Tennessee, and then Alberta, where I became an assistant professor of genetics at the University of Alberta. Each place offered new environments and organisms to explore. But unlike the wilderness of British Columbia, where I had bonded with nature as a young boy, all of my postwar experiences were in areas where people dominated the countryside, and I had to search for the pockets of nature that still flourished.

After an especially cold winter in Edmonton, I accepted a position at the University of British Columbia, in Vancouver, in 1963, returning at last to the city of my birth. With a young family, I repeated the example of my parents, planning camping and fishing trips for my children so that they could experience nature. Every weekend, we would try to get out into a new area, following leads provided by others, driving along country and logging roads around Vancouver to reach isolated rivers and lakes.

I had been at UBC for about a year when I heard about a logging road near Squamish that would take us to a river that was supposed to contain good-sized rainbows. So one Saturday I loaded my children, Tamiko and Troy, into the car and took off for a day trip. Passing Squamish, we left the pavement for a dirt road and soon encountered a sign announcing that we were entering forest company land, where logging trucks had the right of way. The road was in excellent condition and wound through the hills for kilometres. In the area being actively logged, the forest had been cleared and the debris that was left gathered up into great piles to be burned. Having spent most of my life in the east, I wasn't especially disturbed by the logging; after all, I loved working with wood in carpentry and used a lot of paper at work, and I knew that forestry was the engine of the B.C. economy. Besides, the logging roads enabled me to get into remote parts of the province.

When the road finally neared the river, I drove up a hill and found a level spot on the shoulder. We put on our day packs, picked up our fishing gear, and set off. All around us was a combat zone where the soil had been churned up by the tracks of heavy machines, and all that remained of the immense trees were huge stumps and roots that projected at garish angles among the slash. From the top of the hill, the logged-out clearing had looked deceptively smooth and easy to traverse, but once we had left the roadside and started to descend the hill, it became tough slogging to get by the debris. Time after time, I was forced to hoist the children up over obstructions. What I had thought would be an easy ten-minute hike turned into an hour, but once committed, I wasn't about to give up. I kept bantering with the children and playing games with them as we worked our way across the clearing. I was far too focused on the challenge of traversing the clearing to reflect on the fact that this *was* a war zone where human economic demands were conflicting with the continuation of the community of life making up this ecosystem.

It was a sunny day and I soon found myself sweating profusely, kicking myself for not bringing any water and worrying about the children. After much puffing and unjamming of the rods I was carrying from branches and debris, we finally reached the trees at the edge of the logged area. Stepping out of the glare and heat of the clearing and into the dark, cool cathedral of trees was an absolute shock, like stepping from a hot city street into an air-conditioned building. Embraced by the cool shade of the trees, we inhaled the damp, musky odour of vegetation and decaying tree carcasses. We were enfolded in silence. The children immediately stopped bickering and complaining and began to whisper just as if they were in a church. As our eyes adjusted to the shade, we saw that the forest floor was cloaked with moss that smoothed everything into an undulating carpet. The bodies of great leviathans of fallen trees could be seen in outline under the moss, in death nurturing a community of huckleberry, sword ferns, and small trees. As we searched for a trickle of water to drink, the crackling of branches under our feet was muffled by the vegetation. High above us, the canopy stretched to the sky with green branches and needles jockeying for a place in the sun and allowing an ever-shifting filigree of speckled light onto the forest floor. As terrestrial creatures, we could only wonder at the drama of life cycles and predation taking place in the nooks and crannies of the branch tips, needles, and leaves of the canopy and in the soil community hidden beneath our feet. Tamiko, Troy, and I joined hands and reached around the circumference of one of the trees, not even reaching halfway around. Those giants must have been hundreds of years old.

I was dumbstruck. Nature had always been my touchstone, but I had spent much of my life in Ontario, where forests had been heavily impacted and altered by people. There trees had been extracted, creeks rerouted, and the soil cultivated or developed. This was a forest shaped by the forces of nature for ten thousand years, a community of life where death gave birth to new life in an endless recycling of nutrients through the countless species that make up a forest. We had stepped into it from the edge of industrial logging, which would soon transform it into something infinitely simplified and unrecognizable. In those few minutes that my children and I had entered into the forest temple, I had recognized the terrible hubris of the human economy. To transform this matrix of life forms, soil, water, and air into a war zone where soil, air, water, and life were so degraded was a travesty of stewardship and responsibility to future generations. I didn't articulate it that way at the time. I only knew in a profoundly visceral way that industrial logging was not right, that the magnificent forest we had entered was an entity far beyond our comprehension and was worthy of respect and veneration.

I had been set up to have that inspirational encounter with an old-growth forest after reading Rachel Carson's seminal book, *Silent Spring*, in 1962. Years later, I would encounter First Nations people who would educate me about our kinship with other species and the way in which we are all interconnected and interdependent. But that encounter with an ancient forest on the edge of a clear-cut was my moment of enlightenment.

Today, when my grandchildren beg me to go fishing with them, I can't take them to Spanish Banks or the mouth of the Fraser or the Vedder River or other places where my father took me. I can't go back to fish in the Thames River, which is so polluted that people recoil at the thought of eating anything caught there. I can't return to the swamp that soothed me during my adolescence, for it is now covered with an immense shopping mall and parking lot. And the forest that was my epiphany was felled within weeks of my visit there. What remains is my conviction that we must rediscover our biological place and learn to live in balance with the natural world that sustains us.

RICHARD FLANAGAN

Out of a Wild Sea

RICHARD FLANAGAN *was born in Tasmania in 1961.*
His novels, Death of a River Guide, The Sound of One
Hand Clapping, *and* Gould's Book of Fish, *have been
published to acclaim around the world. He also directed
a feature film version of* The Sound of One Hand Clapping,
*which had its world premiere in competition at the 1998 Berlin
Film Festival. He lives in Hobart, Tasmania.*

I HAVE READ TOO MANY BOOKS *on the matter—I hesitate to use a word as precise as* subject—*of man and nature, and at moments of vanity have even visited on a world that had scant need of such one or two more of my own making. For this I ought to ask your forgiveness, but I am hoping you understand. All these books seem to wish to name the unnameable— calling it wilderness or science or spirituality or art—and in so doing somehow seek to limit the limitless cosmos.*

I am heartened as I age by the way animals, birds, fish, friends, trees, grass, and insects move me ever more, whether I come on them in a sidewalk gutter, in a storm-water grate, or in the heart of wild lands. To say nothing of the stars, the sea, and the wind. The shape of clouds. The smell of earth after rain.

I recently camped in the wilderness of the western suburbs of Sydney, in the backyard of a friend for whom I was working as a builder's labourer, and my perception of life was a little altered. Equally improbable are those people I have met whose lives were changed by flying over the wilds of southwest Tasmania. I understand the distinction between the endangered forty-spotted pardalote that flies around my shack, one of the rarest birds in Australia, and a seagull; but I have no time for the snobbery of life that sets one life as superior to another, one experience as greater than the next, that regards the wonder of a woman tending roses as inferior to the wonder of a wilderness zealot atop a remote mountain or in the midst of a river gorge. I know both people and both emotions and regard the two as similar.

Life seems only ever more remarkable, and I am as unaccountably honoured by the sight of a fellow human naked as I was by a seal robbing my fishing net this morning. How to explain the inexplicable in our own nature? Is this gathering of all that is precious to us in speech, books, art—is it all a defence against nothingness, or a celebration of it? Is it an assertion of the soul over chaos, or their necessary reconcilation? Is this, I wonder, what Neruda meant when he asked if there is a greater blessing than to be the ash of which oblivion is made?

As I have grown older I have come to believe in little other than the endless fecundity of stories, which, while ever failing to answer such questions, at least do them honour. Accordingly, when invited to write something for this anthology, I felt I could offer nothing comprehensive, nor large, nor ambitious, far less wise or profound; instead I returned to a story of my own stupidity and its odd consequences, which I wrote several years ago. The only virtue I claim for what follows is truth.

If it fails to entertain, feel free to rip the pages out and use them to roll cigarettes or some-such. The false reverence of books is abominable, one more symptom of an age that no longer reads, and thinks status more important than stories.

I DON'T DRINK OF A MORNING. Not normally. Truth be known, I don't feel the need to drink, not like I once knew the need. And I hadn't meant to be getting drunk that morning. But outside it was a dismal winter's day, and inside the kitchen table miraculously filled with old friends and then food and then bottles, and it steamed with warmth and it smelt of yeast, and none of us had seen each other for such a long time that the only thing flowing more freely than the drink were the stories. Jamma McLeod told a tale about a young man who was discovered in the hugeness of D'Entrecasteaux Channel, heading for the open sea. The young man was in a dinghy with only a bread knife and a loaf of bread, dressed as Desdemona, intending to row the forlorn four hundred miles of ocean that lies between Hobart and Australia because he thought Tasmania was crappy.

I knew a bloke once who tried to do it without a bread knife, said Pig Cranwell.

Everyone laughed. Even me. Even though I was the bloke without the bread knife.

I don't really know why Jim and I wanted to kayak Bass Strait. Sam Jooste was getting married in Sydney and he was our mate, with all that such things meant, and we couldn't afford an airplane ticket. We thought we would just kayak the strait, then hitch from Victoria up to Sydney. At the very least it was a good joke, and consistent with our behaviour to that point, which had established us as people who would kayak any rapid on any river, no matter how big and threatening. A local newspaper ran a photo of us shooting Cataract Gorge in flood with the caption *The Suicide Twins*. That was also a good joke. Some said we had a death wish, but I don't think it was the case.

We had one book with us on the trip, Saul Bellow's *Henderson the Rain King*. It begins like this: "What made me take this trip to Africa? There is no quick explanation. Things got worse and worse and worse and pretty soon they were too complicated." Henderson has a disturbance in his heart, a voice that constantly says, "I want, I want, I want," but what it wants it knows not. Maybe it was like that. On the other hand, maybe if we had a different book, maybe we would have thought about the whole thing differently. I don't know.

Maybe if the weather had been different we would have made it.

No one had predicted anything like the Force Nine gale that turned a calm ocean into a liquid earthquake. The sea grew huge, the waves breaking at the top of their great peaks, crashing into nothingness, to once more rear up as vast molten mountains.

After a time, our initial grim determination gave way to a terrified despair. At some stage we must have realized we might not make it. We activated our emergency radio distress beacon. We may have set off our flares. I can't remember. Nothing happened. No planes, no boats. For hours or minutes or days, nothing. In the middle of Bass Strait, time grew as elastic as the water grew monstrous. Beyond our horror, of course, time maintained its more normal constancy. I know now we spent fourteen hours bobbing around in that wild ocean, little more than heads showing above the water. I was wearing a pair of shorts, a T-shirt, and a life jacket.

At some point, I noticed jets roaring overhead. From so far above we would have been like pieces of dandruff on an enraged giant, impossible to find in the roaring white sea. I waved my arms, knowing it was futile, knowing also that to not do so meant something far worse. Later, much later, I learnt that it was an RAAF squadron of Orions looking for us. All boats in the area that had not headed for safe harbour were also scouring the gale-whipped sea for us.

I could glimpse an island in the distance. Even though the huge waves buffeted me and dragged me and threw me hither and thither, even though my body was senseless with the cold, I kept trying to reach that island. Come what may, I was determined to get there. I succeeded getting close enough that I could distinguish—when momentarily lifted ahigh on the crest of a wave—beaches.

It was just on nightfall when a fishing boat—and whoever those fishermen were, out in such terrible seas, I am profoundly in their debt—finally found and rescued me. They were five minutes away from abandoning their search. That was luck, and without it I would be dead. I sat in the beautiful warmth of their hold next to a throbbing diesel engine as the fishing boat pitched wildly around me, and cared not about anything. After a long time I finally regained enough of my senses to talk some, and I asked how far away was the island. They looked at me blank faced, as though I were even madder than they had first supposed. What island? they asked. There is no landfall within bull's roar of here. Only ocean. I did not weep then.

Somewhere in that ocean, sometime that night, the fishing boat rendezvoused with a police boat, onto which I was transferred. There was Jim, whom they had rescued shortly before I had been found, some miles away from where the fishing boat had discovered me. Jim came up to me and his eyes were fierce and he said, Where's Fin? We've got to find him. We can't give up.

I am Fin, I said finally, for such was my nickname, but he was already gone, demanding of others the same, while somebody followed him around, trying to calm him, to cover him with blankets, to get him to sit down and rest. I heard him say that I was dead, that I was not dead, that I was. Years later I met one of the policemen who had been on that boat. He said that Jim had been in the final stages of hypothermia and that they had expected him to die.

For many years following our trip, whenever I saw that ocean, I used to shiver and feel frightened and feel myself once more a piece of nothingness lost in vastness, seeing nothing but more ocean and an island that didn't exist. No, that's not exactly how it was, though exactly how it was or who I was I no longer know. People ask, though less now, thank God, what it was like, and sometimes I make up a story or two that I think they want to hear, so they will go away satisfied, and sometimes I say more honestly that I don't know, that it was like staring into the sun for a lifetime and feeling forever blinded yet forever sensitive to things no one else can apprehend. Then they go away dissatisfied, annoyed at being told what makes no sense, angry at me whom they think somehow touched. Perhaps rightly, perhaps not.

The people who love me never ask me about it. They are easy about it and sense, as I hope I do with them, the big things that one must be easy about with loved ones. For though we are an age obsessed with telling all, it has to be admitted that most of us understand so little that any attempt at telling all is doomed from the outset. We must glean our truths from the few threshings life leaves us.

I do not remember seeing the sea that much, though it was everywhere and I part of it, falling down waves, floundering, having wave after wave crash over me and wondering when I would surface for my next breath. I do remember a feeling, terrible beyond words, that my soul had abandoned my body, and it was not until I met Majda some years later that I felt my soul returning, though not easily, nor without pain. It returned to me like sensation to a terrible wound. I remember vividly a fear so great and so huge and so empty that you would die to avoid it. I remember also my family and friends coming to me as the ocean howled around me (the noise of the wind and the waves, the screaming and screeching, that too was extraordinary) and I wished to continue seeing them and I knew that for that to happen I had to face this fear and not escape it through death, and I wished for death because it was easier than what I was knowing at the time as life.

Majda and I have kids now—three small girls—and I love them dearly, and when we drive up to visit my brother at Irishtown we come to the point in the road where the land suddenly gives way to the vastness of Bass Strait. A sight wondrous and desolate. A view that jolts. Sometimes one of my girls will say, Did you try and swim that sea, did you, Daddy? and I say, Sort of. Sort of, and they laugh and I laugh, because even to them, more so to them, it is a madness, and it was madness, but I was twenty and Jim was twenty-one and we burnt and we thought we would live forever and we wanted to taunt death, to taste it, and scorn it as only the young feel capable of doing. But it wasn't funny at the time. It wasn't funny for a long, long time afterwards. I didn't laugh for a year or more after it happened. I opened my mouth and raised its corners and made sounds that would be equated with laughter, but nothing was funny. I would lie on the earth like a madman, ear pressed to the ground, and I knew the earth was breathing and me with it and was forever grateful to know such a thing.

Sometimes one of the girls will say, Was it with Jim? Because they know Jim; he comes to our home occasionally when he is not wandering. He tends to arrive back in Tasmania with the spring winds and leaves not long after the first snowfalls of late autumn. He will stand outside with them, bouncing them on the trampoline for ages, and sometimes we talk, but often we don't have much to say. We save words for others. He laughs with the girls and I like that sound, of his and their laughter rising up through the window from the yard outside. I say, Yes, it was with Jim, but it wasn't really, because some hours after the gale blew up and after our pumps failed and our kayaks sank and we were left simply as two specks adrift in that vast churning ocean, the huge waves swept us apart. I did not see him again, not until after I was rescued. Until then, we each thought that the other was dead and that we might also die. We each felt we were to blame, because we had broken the canoeist's golden rule of always staying together. In that eternity between separation and rescue, we each thought we had killed the other.

If Jim were to read this, he would probably think, no, that is not the way it was, and it isn't, but the way it was and is I don't know. Memory and dreams and childhood visions fuse together to form my poor, confused recollection of that long time, long ago, out there in the middle of Bass Strait. To be honest, I can tell you very little of what took place. I only know that what happened was a mystery, that I did not return from the ocean as the foolhardy young man who had entered it.

I also know that I am no longer a solitary speck in a huge wild ocean. My life is crowded now. I became a writer, but that's not what is so important to me. Sometimes, not very often now, one of our girls finds me alone, crying. And she asks me, why? I clutch her tight, as if she were a fisherman hauling me out of a wild sea. And I shiver, and I say, I don't know why. I just am.

Acknowledgments

"The Requiem Shark" is based on a passage in *The Shark Net* by Robert Drewe, Viking Penguin, 2000.

"The Same River Twice: Stenothermal Waters and the Remorseless Flow of Time" by David Quammen is modified from an essay that appeared in *Outside* magazine in May 1986. Reprinted by permission of David Quammen. All rights reserved. Copyright © 1986 and 2002 by David Quammen.

"The Day the Waylakas Dance" is modified from a passage in *Light at the Edge of the World* by Wade Davis. Copyright © 2001 by Wade Davis. Used by permission of the author and Douglas & McIntyre.

"The Deer in Springtime" is modified from an essay in *Cultivating Delight* by Diane Ackerman. Copyright © 2001 by Diane Ackerman. Used by permission of the author and HarperCollins.

"Out of a Wild Sea" is modified from an original essay first published by *Age* newspaper in 1995, and as part of *The Penguin Book of Death* published by Penguin Books in 1997. Copyright © 1995 by Richard Flanagan. Reprinted with modifications by permission of the author.